Lesson Planning

A RESEARCH-BASED MODEL FOR K–12 CLASSROOMS

Melinda K. Schoenfeldt

Ball State University

Denise E. Salsbury

Ball State University

PEARSON
Merrill
Prentice Hall

Upper Saddle River, New Jersey
Columbus, Ohio

Library of Congress Cataloging-in-Publication Data

Schoenfeldt, Melinda K.
   Lesson planning : a research-based model for K–12 classrooms/Melinda K. Schoenfeldt,
Denise E. Salsbury.
      p. cm.
   Includes bibliographical references and index.
   ISBN-13: 978-0-13-173594-1 (pbk.)
   ISBN-10: 0-13-173594-2 (pbk.)
   1. Lesson planning.   I. Salsbury, Denise E.   II. Title.
LB1027.4.S357 2009
371.3—dc22

                                                                2007041777

**Vice President and Executive
   Publisher:** Jeffery W. Johnston
Editor: Darcy Betts Prybella
Editorial Assistant: Nancy Holstein
Production Editor: Mary Harlan
Production Coordination: Thistle Hill
   Publishing Services, LLC

Photo Coordinator: Sandra Schaefer
Design Coordinator: Diane C. Lorenzo
Cover Design: Jeff Vanik
Cover Image: Fotosearch
Production Manager: Susan Hannahs
Director of Marketing: David Gesell
Marketing Coordinator: Brian Mounts

This book was set in Bookman by Integra Software Services. It was printed and bound by R.R.
Donnelley & Sons Company. The cover was printed by R.R. Donnelley & Sons Company.

Photo credits: Provided by the E. C. Schoenfeldt family, p. 2 (left); Anthony Magnacca/
Merrill, pp. 2 (right), 58 (right); Krista Greco/Merrill, p. 20; Kathy Kirtland/Merrill, p. 32;
EMG Education Management Group, p. 44; Silver Burdett Ginn, p. 58 (left); Frank Siteman/
PhotoEdit Inc., p. 76; Denise E. Salsbury, p. 98; Maria B. Vonada/Merrill, p. 114 (left);
Copyright 2001–2007 SMART Technologies Inc., all rights reserved, p. 114 (right).

Pearson Education Ltd.
Pearson Education Singapore Pte. Ltd.
Pearson Education Canada, Ltd.
Pearson Education–Japan

Pearson Education Australia Pty. Limited
Pearson Education North Asia Ltd.
Pearson Educación de Mexico, S.A. de C.V.
Pearson Education Malaysia Pte. Ltd.

10 9 8 7 6 5 4 3 2 1
ISBN-13: 978-0-13-173594-1
ISBN-10:   0-13-173594-2

About the Authors

Melinda K. Schoenfeldt, Ph.D.

Melinda Schoenfeldt earned her doctorate in curriculum and instruction from Kansas State University. Prior to earning her doctorate, Schoenfeldt taught elementary, middle, and high school courses in public and private schools. She is now an associate professor in the Department of Elementary Education at Ball State University. While at Ball State, she has taught undergraduate courses in lesson planning and classroom management, in addition to supervising student teachers in the United States and Germany. She has also served as the faculty coordinator and instructor of study abroad programs in England, Denmark, and Mexico. Schoenfeldt won a dissertation award from the National Council for Geographic Education, was a visiting scholar in geography education at Silkeborg Seminarium in Silkeborg, Denmark, was a fellow at the Virginia Ball Center for Creative Inquiry, and is currently an Enhancing Student Learning Initiative fellow. Schoenfeldt is one of three members of the Learning Assessment Model Project (LAMP) development team. LAMP won the 2005 Christa McAuliffe Award for Excellence in Teacher Education. She currently serves as Teachers College iTunes University Faculty Liaison, teaches graduate courses in Ball State University's online master's degree program in elementary education, teaches doctoral seminars, and chairs the university's committee of the European Teacher Education Network.

Denise E. Salsbury, Ph.D.

Denise Salsbury is an assistant professor at Ball State University in the Department of Elementary Education of the Teachers College, where she teachers instructional planning, classroom management, and integration of educational technology in core curriculum courses. She has taught elementary grades K–6, specifically fourth grade for ten years, and has served as a school integrated librarian. Her teaching position presented many opportunities to write thematic science and social studies curriculum for the school district. Her first degree is in music education. Salsbury completed her doctoral program at Kansas State University in curriculum and instruction with an emphasis in both elementary social studies and geography education. While in Kansas, she was an active member and officer of the Kansas Geographic Alliance, which gave her the opportunity to attend geographic education and leadership institutes at the National Geographic Society. Salsbury has presented at National Council for Geographic Education (NCGE) annual meetings, won a NCGE dissertation award, and is currently chair of the Geography Literacy Task Force (subcommittee of the NCGE Curriculum and Instruction Committee).

Preface

Thoughtful lesson planning is essential for good teaching and student learning to take place. It is an "unseen" and underappreciated skill of professional educators. If you watch an experienced teacher, you see how the lesson seems to flow. If you stop to think carefully about what you are watching, you'll begin to notice evidence of planning. A well-conceived and well-written plan indicates that a teacher has thought through the lesson and has carefully crafted one that will help students master new content, concepts, and skills.

Lesson Planning: A Research-Based Model for K–12 Classrooms guides teachers through the development of standards-based lesson plans. In addition, this book emphasizes research-based practice. The lesson planning process in this book guides a teacher in the selection of research-based instructional strategies and types of materials, all designed to consider all learners' needs. The plan elements themselves are based in research as well.

The purpose of *Lesson Planning: A Research-Based Model for K–12 Classrooms* is clearly identified in the book's title. We envision the book being used primarily in undergraduate education classes as the main text in a lesson planning course or as a supplemental text in methods or other pedagogy courses. The book could also be used in alternative licensure programs and in in-service or workshop settings.

The book is divided into two parts. Part I establishes the theoretical foundation of the ideas used in the lesson planning process described in Part II.

- Chapter 1, "Planning Is Necessary," provides a myriad of reasons that lesson planning is necessary, supporting each with current and historically significant educational research. The lesson planning process and lesson plan formats are introduced.

- Chapter 2, "Teaching Is Informed Decision Making," establishes the idea that teachers are professional decision makers who use research to inform and support their decisions. In addition, the chapter looks at and explains the foundational concepts and beliefs used throughout the text.

Part II is a step-by-step guide to developing direct and inquiry-based lesson plans.

- Chapter 3, "Identifying a Topic and Academic Standards," explains the beginning point of the planning process and emphasizes the importance of standards-based plans.

- Chapter 4, "Writing Lesson Goals and Objectives," examines the importance of the various types of objectives and explains how to write each type.
- Chapter 5, "Designing Formative and Summative Assessments," stresses the importance of creating assessments during the planning process, after writing lesson objectives, rather than creating assessments after instruction has begun. Various types of assessments are explained.
- Chapter 6, "Choosing the Lesson Content and Instructional Strategies," guides the reader in becoming knowledgeable in both academic content and "best practice."
- Chapter 7, "Selecting Lesson Materials," helps the reader understand the importance of selecting materials to meet the needs of the diverse learners in a classroom and guides readers in how to select them.
- Chapter 8, "Creating a Lesson Plan," provides samples of, and directions for creating, both direct instruction and inquiry-based lesson plans.

There are several recurring features in *Lesson Planning: A Research-Based Model for K–12 Classrooms*. Though the main focus of this book is on creating a lesson plan for a single lesson, in reality classroom teaching uses interdisciplinary units. Each of the chapters in Part II contain boxed **Unit Connections**, which explain how the chapter's content is used in the development of a unit.

Technology affects every facet of life today. So, another recurring feature is the technology tie-in, **Technology in Education**, abbreviated **TiE**. Web sites cited in this feature extend the professional concepts discussed in the book and provide practical help in the lesson planning process. These include rubric generating sites, lesson plan templates, ideas for lesson activities, and links to useful classroom materials such as printable manipulatives and graphic organizers.

One of the best ways to become more proficient as a teacher is to talk with other teachers. The **Reality Check** feature in each chapter provides advice from practicing classroom teachers. These teachers from across the United States, representing a range of subjects and grade levels, weigh in on key points in each chapter.

Meeting the needs of all learners is extremely important. Considering the diverse needs of students is woven into the content of every chapter. So, too, are the INTASC principles. Connections are made to these principles in both chapter content and activities.

Because this text is a guide to creating a lesson plan, the **Your Turn** feature at the end of each chapter is designed to actively involve the reader in the lesson planning process. By the end of the book, readers will have created their own standards-based lesson plan in both direct and indirect instruction formats.

ACKNOWLEDGMENTS

The planning process, information, and ideas presented in *Lesson Planning: A Research-Based Model for K–12 Classrooms* have been used with thousands of preservice practicum students and student teachers. We thank them, their supervising classroom teachers, and our university colleagues for helping us refine the planning process and activities.

We would also like to thank the talented professional educators who answered our questions and provided inspiration and practical advice. Thanks to Dru Clarke, Jill Carson-Coen, Terri Durgan, Bryan Fountain, Pat Gillespie, Matthew Huber, Alea Lafond, Barbara Martin, Sarah Miller, Melissa Milius, Dennis Rees, Dutch Schoenfeldt, Carrie Smith, Jolena Sutherland, Michelle Sutton, Jennifer Weesner, Amanda Williams, Linda Williams, and Alyson Woodruff.

The authors would also like to thank the following reviewers: Diane Bressner, Palm Beach Community College; Dale Campbell, Jacksonville State University; Elaine Pierce Chakonas, Northeastern Illinois University; Kim Hall, Coastal Carolina University, Northcentral University; Bruno Hicks, University of McFort Kent; Gae Johnson, Northern Arizona University; Cherrie Kassem, Ramapo College of New Jersey; Marie Lassmann, Texas A & M University–Kingsville; Barbara Mize, Barton College; and Harriet P. Sturgeon, University of Houston–Clear Lake.

Brief Contents

Contents

PART TWO
Structural Foundations of a Lesson Plan 31

Choosing the Lesson Content and Instructional Strategies   77

Note: Every effort has been made to provide accurate and current Internet information in this book. However, the Internet and information on it are constantly changing, so it is inevitable that some of the Internet addresses listed in this textbook will change.

PART I

Conceptual Foundations
for Planning a Lesson

Planning Is Necessary

Objective: Understand the importance of planning.

1.1 List two reasons that teachers create lesson plans.

1.2 Write a personal goal for creating lesson plans.

Relevant INTASC Principles: #6, #9 (See inside back cover of this book for list of INTASC Principles.)

PLANNING IS PROFESSIONAL DECISION MAKING

When you discover your mission, you will feel its demand. It will fill you with enthusiasm and a burning desire to get to work on it.

—W. Clement Stone

Most of us have been to the doctor's office many times, recognize some basic symptoms as indications of certain ailments, and know how to treat many ailments ourselves. But we certainly recognize that we aren't doctors. Many people possess a lot of knowledge, love children, spent many years in school themselves, and have taught someone how to do something. They may know a bit about teaching, much as most of us know a bit about medicine. But loving children and possessing a lot of knowledge don't make them professional educators. Just as doctors and other professionals have a specific body of knowledge and set of skills, so too do professional educators. Planning for instruction is one of those skills. In fact, careful lesson planning is arguably more important now than at any time in the history of American education.

TEACHER ACCOUNTABILITY: PAST AND PRESENT

Learn from the past, dream about the future.

—Donald Trump

Demands on teachers have changed tremendously during America's history. For example, being a teacher in a colonial school did not require formal training. Teaching meant requiring children to memorize and recite facts and using corporal punishment to maintain order (Kaestle, 1983).

Public education, defined as education that is mandated by the government and paid for in part or in whole through taxes (Mondale, 2002), began in America in the mid-nineteenth century. Teachers were expected to teach what is commonly referred to as the three R's: reading, (w)riting (actually penmanship), and (a)rithmetic. In addition, these schools were expected to teach children how to get along with each other and to become productive, responsible citizens (Morrison, 2000). Recitation, drilling, and oral quizzes were the main instructional strategies.

Schools were generally open only a few months of the year, usually when the children were not needed to work at home or on the farm. Students of all ages and ability levels were taught in one-room schoolhouses, by one teacher. During this time, normal schools for teacher training were begun. These were often two-year programs.

One of the biggest challenges confronting American education today is how to respond to increasing demands for teacher accountability. A look at the 10 INTASC (Interstate New Teacher Assessment and Support Consortium) Principles (Council of Chief State School Officers, 1992), which are listed on the inside back cover of this book, reveals the demands placed on teachers. The standards identify the basic common knowledge and skills teachers should have and new teachers must acquire before they can obtain a teaching license. Now, in the 21st century, teachers must have

TECHNOLOGY IN EDUCATION

For an interesting multimedia overview of the **history of American education** go to http://www.pbs.org/kcet/publicschool/index.html.

For a free copy of *Education in the United States: A Brief Overview,* go to http://www.edpubs.org/webstore/Content/search.asp.

For information on IDEA and NCLB, go to http://www.ed.gov.

specialized training and a university degree. Schools are governed by local school boards. They receive the bulk of their funding from state and local taxes, but also must meet federal guidelines including those set out in IDEA and NCLB. The Individuals with Disabilities Education Act (IDEA) (U.S. Department of Education, 2005b), regulates education for students with disabilities. The No Child Left Behind Act (NCLB) (U.S. Department of Education, 2003, 2005a, 2007) regulates school accountability issues, including a mandate that teachers be highly qualified and that schools must demonstrate and provide documentation of adequate yearly progress of student learning.

Conceptual changes regarding the nature of teaching and learning have led to the development of standards for teacher candidates and the institutions that prepare them. An important feature embedded throughout the National Council for Accreditation of Teacher Education (NCATE) standards is the expectation that teacher candidates be able to demonstrate that they actually have an impact on their students' learning. NCATE defines itself on its home Web site as "the [teaching] profession's mechanism to help establish high quality teacher preparation" (2006). This increased focus on teacher competence is unparalleled in America's educational history.

Planning is essential for good teaching and student learning to take place. It is an "unseen" and underappreciated element, much like many of the skills possessed by professionals in all fields, and yet planning demonstrates a teacher's competence. If you watch an experienced teacher, you see that the lesson seems to flow. If you stop to think carefully about what you are watching, you'll begin to notice evidence of planning. Students are seated in a specific arrangement, materials are ready to be handed out to students, the teacher knows the topic's content, and so on. The teacher planned all of that and more before stepping in front of the students.

 ## Reality Check

Question: How do you respond to the comment that "real teachers" don't write lesson plans?

I do not write the detailed plans required at most universities, but had I not learned to write those I would not consider all those things that go into a well-planned lesson when filling out a plan book. I try to make notes of which standards I am using as I write in my plan book, and in my mind I have my objectives, goals, essential questions, and assessments (whether informal or formal). Without those college lesson plans I would probably not have many of those components anywhere in my mind.

Amanda Williams
Westview Elementary Kindergarten

PLANNING AS ROAD TRIP ANALOGY

Lesson planning involves making a lot of decisions. Perhaps it will be helpful to use a road trip as an analogy. Imagine taking a road trip from Kansas City, Missouri, to Denver, Colorado. If you look at the map in Figure 1.1, or visualize one mentally, you'll realize that to get to Denver from Kansas City means you'll travel through the state of Kansas from east to west. Look at the following lists. The lesson planning elements are compared to the decisions needed for taking a successful, well-planned road trip.

Planning a Lesson	*Planning a Trip*
Topic	Deciding on type of trip
Standards	Road map
Lesson goal	Determine a reason
Lesson objective	Choose a specific destination
Lesson content	Travel guides
Lesson materials	Items to pack
Lesson plan	Itinerary
Implementation/ teaching lesson	Taking the trip
Assessment	Scrapbook

Lesson planning elements in the list will be explained in detail throughout this book. To help you conceptualize planning, each chapter continues the analogy between lesson planning and the road trip. Thoughtful decisions are made when planning a lesson plan or a road trip, and both are affected by the knowledge and skills of the person who is doing the planning.

Good plans shape good decisions.

—Lester R. Bittel

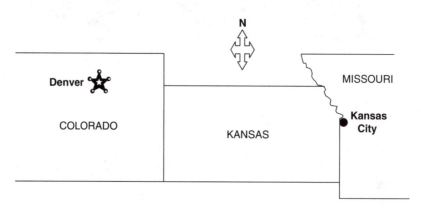

FIGURE 1.1 Planning a Road Trip

REASONS FOR PLANNING

Careful lesson planning serves several purposes. Planning brings focus and organization to a lesson, helps a teacher stay on topic during instruction, helps a teacher select appropriate materials and teaching strategies, ensures that academic standards will be addressed, helps with classroom management, and helps a teacher to become a more reflective practitioner. Planning provides teachers with confidence and security (Clark & Yinger, 1979; Kauchak & Eggen, 2003). A well-written plan indicates that a teacher has thought through the lesson and has carefully crafted a lesson that will help students master new content, concepts, and skills.

Exemplary teaching occurs when teachers have taken the time to prepare themselves to stand in front of a group of students of varied learning abilities and provide instruction. Progressive teachers adopt and adapt skills of "observation, interviews, questionnaires, collecting and interpreting artifacts and performances" (Zemelman, Daniels, & Hyde, 2005, p. 252) while monitoring students' academic growth; all of this, and more, is not possible without a lot of planning. Preparation before beginning a presentation and transmission of content keeps teachers from becoming overwhelmed, distracted, or unfocused on the lesson's end results (Burden & Byrd, 2003). It is easier to stand in the classroom prepared than trying to wing it in front of a group of students.

Lesson Focus

A successful lesson requires focus. Setting clear lesson goals and objectives creates focus and direction. This seems obvious, and yet researchers report that teachers do not typically start the planning process with goals and objectives in mind, but rather by collecting interesting activities, content, or materials (McCutcheon, 1980; Mintz, 1979; Peterson, Marx, & Clark, 1978; Starko et al., 2003). Although interesting activities and materials can be important to a successful lesson, they do not in and of themselves bring clear focus to a lesson.

Remember our lesson plan as a road trip analogy? A lesson is not merely a series of interesting activities strung together to fit the available time, any more than the successful completion of a planned road trip is a series of unrelated small journeys. We're headed to Denver on our road trip. Let's say that a friend tells us he knows a great restaurant only an hour's drive from Kansas City. We decide to stop there for lunch, only to find that it takes us miles off the interstate, adding extra time to our trip. Even though the drive was nice and the restaurant was indeed great, we are no nearer to Denver, our intended destination. Activities can work this way as well. Though they may be interesting, they may not take our students in the right direction. There are other activities, just as there will be other good restaurants, that we can select that will also help us reach our intended goal.

Remaining Focused During Instruction

Don't agonize. Organize.

—Florynce Kennedy

Researchers have found a positive correlation between the number of planning statements teachers made and their tendency to remain focused on the topic they were teaching (Peterson et al., 1978). The lesson plan helps the teacher stay organized and on topic. At one school, the students hold a short pep assembly every year to hand out various teacher awards voted on by the students themselves. One of those awards is for the teacher easiest to get off-topic. Getting off-topic is easy to do. Students often ask questions that are only marginally relevant to the current topic. Students also like to relate personal anecdotes during lessons. These may or may not be directly related to the lesson's topic. If a teacher takes a "detour" to allow for these stories or to answer the somewhat off-topic question, it is important to get back "on track" as quickly as possible. Having a well-planned lesson can help a teacher do just that with a quick glance back at the written plan. It is also realistic and often desirable to tell students before you begin a lesson that you will provide a short time at the end of the lesson for personal stories and additional questions, and then reinforce that point when the questions and stories arise.

Sometimes, though, it is important to take "detours." A short detour won't usually take too much time and may be an interesting diversion. In a lesson, these detours are referred to as **teachable moments,** unplanned opportunities to broaden the scope of the lesson and to allow students to make personal connections to the content. Often children are trying to make sense of the new information by tying it to prior experience. They may also be trying to find the meaning of the new information, the personal relevance of it. If new information does not make sense or have personal relevance, the probability of this new information being learned is extremely low (Sousa, 2001). You are in the driver's seat and make the decisions that you feel are in the best interest of your students' learning.

Selecting Appropriate Materials and Strategies

Learning should be intentional, not incidental. Teachers intend certain things to be learned during a lesson (refer to Figure 1.2). The chart in Figure 1.2 outlines the lesson planning process described throughout this text. Each chapter in Part II will explain each step in greater detail. For now, refer to the chart to help you understand that lesson planning has a process and order.

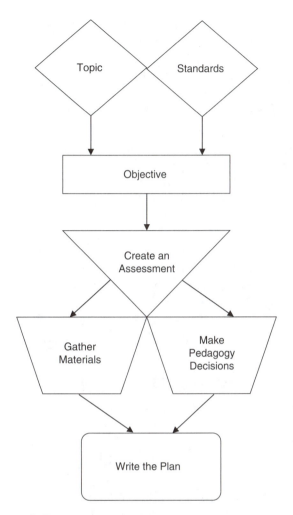

FIGURE 1.2   Lesson Planning Process

At the beginning of the planning process a teacher should ask, "What do I want my students to know or be able to do?" The answers to that question provide the ideas for the lesson's goals and objectives, which in turn create the lesson's focus. Lesson activities and materials are selected after goals and objectives are written. These activities and materials are intentionally designed into the lesson because they will increase student learning of the intended content. If activities were selected before objectives were written, learning might take place, but it would be incidental rather than intentional.

Too often teachers think all learning must be fun. Learning is not always entertaining, certainly not like a movie or a day at an amusement park. "Learning can be engaging, engrossing, amazing, disorienting, involving, and often deeply pleasurable. If it's fun, fine. But it doesn't need to be fun" (Ayers, 1993, p. 13). A person could explain it this way, "I recall learning to ride a bicycle. I fell many times before I learned to keep the bike upright without training wheels. I suffered many scraped knees, elbows, and shins.

I had bruises all over. Riding my bike was a lot of fun *after* I learned how. The learning *process* for me, however, was frustrating, engrossing, and challenging, but not fun."

During the lesson planning process, it is important to select materials and teaching strategies that will help the students learn the new skill or knowledge in an effective way. Those may be enjoyable for the students, but fun is not the most important criterion in the selection process. Student motivation *is* important, though. The bike rider explained, "I was highly motivated to learn to ride a bike because once I did I could ride to the nearby park with my friends, so I stuck with it even through bruises, scrapes, and gravel in my knee."

Brophy (1998) defines motivation to learn as the "tendency to find academic activities meaningful and worthwhile and to try to get the intended learning benefits from them" (p. 12). Sullo (2007) encapsulates the theory of motivation as an attempt by humans to make sense of their world. So during the planning process, select your materials and strategies with the idea of motivating, rather than merely entertaining, your students. Select materials that will help your students make connections between their learning and real life.

Incorporating Academic Standards

National and state academic content standards have been identified for all subject areas. Academic content standards indicate what students should know and be able to do in each of those subject areas. For example, Standard 4 of the National Standards for the English Language Arts states, "Students adjust their use of spoken, written, and visual language (e.g., conventions, style, vocabulary) to communicate effectively with a variety of audiences and for different purposes" (National Council of Teachers of English, 1996). To clarify the standard, look at key terms stating what students should know ("use of spoken, written, and visual language") and be able to do ("communicate effectively"). Standards across all subject areas identify the core concepts that should be taught within grade level–assigned curriculum.

Recent research (EdSource, 2006) has shown that implementing a coherent, standards-based instructional program is one of the four school practices most strongly correlated with higher academic performance scores. It is important, then, for teachers to use the academic standards for their given grade level to design lessons for their students. During the planning process, specific standards can help a teacher determine a direction for a lesson. But a teacher can choose whatever methods are found appropriate to help the students meet the standards.

Classroom Management

"Students who are interested and involved in the academic work at hand are less likely to daydream, disrupt, and defy" (Weinstein &

Reality Check

Question: How do you respond to the statement that "real teachers" don't write lesson plans?

I have to confess that as an undergrad education major, I often complained about the detailed form required for lesson plans in our practicum classes. Murmurs from classmates like "Real teachers don't write lesson plans" could always be heard. Now that I am a "real teacher" with my own class and my own students, I have to admit that my lesson plans are not always written out. But just because plans aren't written in a detailed format with specific requirements on a daily basis, doesn't mean that I don't think through those steps!

In fact, I found that during my first year of teaching, I *did* spend a great deal of time planning lessons. For me, the thinking process is the most important part of planning. I'd usually jot down phrases or brief descriptions of the activities for each day and the progression my lesson would take. I still often thought about all the key lesson components such as motivating students, establishing my purpose/objective for the lesson, and a plan for assessing. So although it is true that I do not write down every detail of a lesson when I plan, I do spend time establishing a purpose and choosing the most effective way to accomplish that.

Carrie Smith
Prairie Vista Elementary School
Fourth- and fifth-grade multiage

Mignano, 2007, p. 225). In other words, classroom management and student motivation are closely linked. Motivating students doesn't happen accidentally. You need to intentionally decide to make student motivation an integral part of every lesson plan.

One way to motivate learners is to use variety—variety in materials, teaching techniques, questioning, assessment, and so on. Deliberate use of variety, in other words, planning it into lessons, has been shown by researchers (Kintsch & Bates, 1977; Napell, 1978; Saurino, Saurino, & See, 2002; Williams & Ware, 1977) to be a critical factor in effective classrooms. Variety keeps students interested, and students interested in lessons are less likely to misbehave. Experienced teachers are much more interested in preventing misbehavior—being proactive—than reacting to it after it occurs. Jones and Jones (1995) found that proactive management techniques can reduce disruptive behavior by at least 75%.

Being a Reflective Practitioner

Reflection is a teacher's attempt to determine whether she accomplished what she set out to do and to determine if there are more effective ways to accomplish the original goals (National Research Council, 2000). After observing student teachers teach a lesson, one supervisor reports that she wants them to reflect on their teaching experience and planning, and usually asks them, "How did the lesson go? What would you do the same next time, and what would you change and why?" To find the answers to those questions, let's look at the responses of two different student teachers. Let's call them Pat and Chris.

Pat   The lesson went really well. The students were having fun with the manipulatives. I'm glad I put them in groups to work, too. That way everyone could learn from the others. I would definitely use those ideas again. I wouldn't change anything.

Chris   The lesson went really well. Each group solved all the problems I gave them in the allotted time. The students enjoyed using the manipulatives. But I noticed that in one group, Kevin hogged most of the manipulatives. Sarah was in that group, and she is very quiet and didn't speak up about needing some of the manipulatives. I think I'd give each student a set of manipulatives next time, and I'll make sure to be more selective in who works in what group. I also might let students work alone for a bit before putting them in groups. I think some of the children who take longer to think through problems just let the faster ones solve the problems for the group. I want students learning from each other, but I really want everyone to solve at least one problem on their own. So I'd keep the manipulatives and group work, but I'd make the changes I mentioned.

Though Chris and Pat had made similar decisions in designing their lessons, it is easy to see that Chris was much more reflective about his practice after instruction. He delved more deeply into evaluating the learning situation.

Reflection allows teachers to evaluate an experience, learn from mistakes, repeat successful strategies, and revise for future instruction. Reflection helps teachers become more thoughtful and deliberate in their decision making while planning for instruction (Bean, Fulmer, Zigmond, & Grumet, 1995).

Reality Check

Question: Do experienced teachers write lesson plans?

Writing complete lesson plans should be mandatory for new teachers, but after a while I feel a veteran teacher can take shortcuts because it becomes second nature. New teachers need to assimilate the process. I also think lesson plans should be completely written out for emergency substitute lesson plans.

Barbara Martin
Teachers Consultant
Arizona Geographic Alliance

LONG-RANGE PLANNING

Once you are in your own classroom, you will be expected to plan lessons for an entire school year. To begin the process, most teachers sit down with the school or district curriculum guide for their grade level, the class textbooks, and state standards. By looking through these resources, teachers can develop a list of topics and create a general outlined sequence. They might then organize the sequence into quarters or grading periods. Then the teacher needs to decide how many weeks each topic will require within the grading period, perhaps noting topics that might be enhanced with the use of field study, special activities, or guest speakers.

From that general outline structure, a teacher can begin to outline each week and plan individual days. The daily lessons are the first time the teacher will make more detailed plans. See Figure 1.3 for an example of a teacher's year-long outline for fifth-grade social studies. This teacher's school year is 180 days and is divided into 4 grading periods or terms.

 ## *Reality Check*

Question: Do experienced teachers write lesson plans?

I write complete lesson plans when creating new lessons and units.

Dennis Rees
Peoria USD
Sixth grade

 # TECHNOLOGY IN EDUCATION

To see examples of **long-range plans** online, go to http://assist.educ.msu.edu/ASSIST/classroom/activities2/II_Year_Long_Plan/ElBroadGoals.htm.

To see examples of **unit plans,** go to http://www.eduref.org/cgi-bin/lessons.cgi/Interdisciplinary. Or http://fcit.usf.edu/holocaust/activity/Intermed.htm.

To see examples of daily lesson plans, go to http://school.discovery.com/lessonplans/. Or http://www.eduref.org/Virtual/Lessons/index.shtml. Or http://www.pbs.org/teachersource/.

First Term (45 days/9 weeks) Topics

1. Early Explorers to North America (3 weeks)
   Map and globe skills
2. Native American Culture (3 weeks)
   Possible field trip to Native American Heritage Center
3. Colonial American Life (3 weeks)
   Divide class into thirds; simulate life as northern, middle, and southern colonists

Second Term (45 days/9 weeks) Topics

1. The American Revolutionary Period (3 weeks)
2. Forming Our Governing System (3 weeks)
   Set up class government to parallel American system
3. Basic Economic Principles (3 weeks)

Third Term (45 days/9 weeks) Topics

1. Westward Expansion (3 weeks)
2. The Civil War (3 weeks)
3. Immigration (3 weeks)
   Family histories

Fourth Term (45 days/9 weeks) Topics

1. Technological Change (3 weeks)
   Visit the Museum of Science and Industry
2. Examination of the Twentieth Century by Decades (4 weeks)
   Interviews of people alive in the 1950s forward
3. The Twenty-First Century (2 weeks)
   Global interdependence activity

FIGURE 1.3 Long-Range Plan for Fifth-Grade Social Studies

DAILY LESSON PLANS

Parts of a Daily Lesson

In your teacher preparation courses and during your practicum experiences in schools, you may see and be required to use a variety of lesson plan formats. All of them, however, have a beginning, middle, and end and are designed to help you organize effective instruction for your students. It is important when creating a lesson plan to organize the learning experience so that the lesson develops concepts and ideas in a logical progression from simple to complex, concrete to abstract. In most formats, the beginning of a lesson is used to gain the students' attention, let the students know the lesson's objectives and expectations of them, and help the teacher determine the prior experience of each student with the topic's content. Often, teachers discover during this part of the lesson that some of the students have misconceptions about the topic and will be able to correct those ideas before moving on to the lesson's specifics. For example, Ms. Webb was beginning a lesson that would involve using the cardinal directions. She wanted the students to label the cardinal directions in the classroom and handed out the N, S, W, and E to 4 children. The little boy with the N wanted to place it on the ceiling because he "knew" that north was "up."

The middle part of a lesson contains the "heart" or "body" of the lesson. This part of a direct instruction lesson plan must be logically organized so that students will see the relationships between the major concepts or ideas within the lesson. It is important that this part of the lesson incorporate enough examples, illustrations, and opportunities for students to experiment with and practice the content. The lesson plan format in this book will help you create a cohesive lesson plan body that includes teacher modeling, guided practice, independent practice, and checking for understanding.

The end of a lesson is often called **closure.** This provides an opportunity for the teacher to determine the level of understanding of each student and allows for a review of the lesson's main points. This is one more chance for a teacher to clear up misconceptions.

If a teacher decides to use an inquiry method, sometimes called *discovery* or *problem solving,* the lesson will still have a beginning, middle, and end. The beginning is still used to focus attention on the lesson's topic and content and to access prior experience and knowledge. During this stage, students list one or more questions that they would like to explore. During the body of the lesson, students gather data through various means; reading and experimenting, for example. They then organize and interpret the data to provide a possible answer to the question posed in the lesson's beginning.

Teachers are facilitating learning by directing students to useful materials, checking understanding through questioning, and providing direct instruction of skills when needed. During the lesson's closure, or end, students reflect on their experience through various means, which could include journaling or creation of some product such as an essay, model, poem, mural, or other drawing. The teacher can use this end product as a form of assessment of student learning. This book will help you create lesson plans for this type of lesson as well.

INTERDISCIPLINARY THEMATIC UNIT

A teacher may plan to spend more than one day teaching a particular topic. In fact, that is quite common. Sometimes, a teacher decides to take a topic and build a series of lessons that connect the topic's content with more than one subject area. A **thematic unit** is instruction built around a central theme, concept, or topic. An **interdisciplinary thematic unit** is instruction built around

UNIT CONNECTION

A unit is a series of lessons connected by a single topic. Units of instruction can last for one week or much longer. A distinguishing characteristic of a unit is that it is interdisciplinary; it includes content from more than one subject area.

Topic: Natural disasters
Subject Areas: Science, social studies, language arts

Week 1:

Science: Types of natural disasters: tornadoes, hurricanes, earthquakes, typhoons, volcanic eruptions
Social Studies: Mapping highest concentration of each type of disaster
Language Arts: Read stories about surviving a natural disaster. Write journal entries from the perspective of a survivor.

one basic theme that includes two or more disciplines (Roberts & Kellough, 2008).

In self-contained elementary classrooms, integration of subjects is a fairly easy process because the classroom teacher teaches most, if not all, of the content subjects. In middle and high school classes, or in upper elementary school classes that are departmentalized, teachers who teach various subjects may or may not plan together to create interdisciplinary units. See the Unit Connection box in this chapter for a partial list of possible interdisciplinary connections for the topic of natural disasters.

Once a topic is decided on, the teachers follow the same planning process as they would for creating individual lessons: writing objectives, gathering content information and lesson materials, creating assessments, selecting instructional strategies, and planning activities. Teachers then create their daily lesson plans, making sure to connect their subject areas to the others' content. Usually, too, an interdisciplinary thematic unit will have a culminating activity at the end of the unit as the closure for the unit, as well as a summative assessment.

IN SUMMARY

Planning is essential for good teaching and student learning to take place. Careful lesson planning serves several purposes. Planning brings focus to a lesson and helps the teacher stay on track during instruction; helps the teacher select appropriate materials and teaching strategies and organize them in a logical order; is a proactive strategy to use in preventing student misbehavior; ensures that standards are included; and helps a teacher to become a more reflective practitioner.

YOUR TURN

ACTIVITY: Reflections on Planning

INTASC Principles 9 and 10

Directions:

1. In the following space or on another piece of paper, list two reasons for creating lesson plans that you recall from reading Chapter 1.

    a.

    b.

2. Think about something for which you had to plan ahead. For this exercise, choose something other than planning to teach someone something. Perhaps you planned a surprise birthday party for a friend or relative, planned and cooked a special dinner, or planned a trip. Create an outline here or on a separate sheet of paper that shows the steps you took. Also list what you learned about doing the same thing the next time. What did you forget to plan for?

    I planned _____ .

    a.

    b.

    c.

    If I planned this same activity again, I would remember to:

3. Now think about a memorable lesson when you were an elementary, middle, or high school student. In the space provided here for My "Remembered" Lesson or on a separate piece of paper, list the lesson's topic, as many of the materials as you can, how the teacher began the lesson, what you did during the lesson, and how you demonstrated to the teacher that you had learned what she wanted you to learn.

My "Remembered" Lesson

Lesson Topic:

Grade:

Materials the teacher had us use (e.g., a computer, paint, etc.):

Lesson activities I remember doing during the lesson:

How I **demonstrated my learning:**

4. Share your remembered lesson in a small group of at least two other people. Compare the lessons by filling in the chart here or on another piece of paper. Discuss why you think the remembered lessons have things in common. What makes a lesson memorable? How will you use this information when you plan your own lesson?

COMPARISON OF REMEMBERED LESSONS

Similarities	Differences

Evidence of Planning by Your Teachers

5. In your group, create a list of things that, upon reflection, you know the teachers planned ahead in order to teach the lessons.

6. Do you think your teachers' reasons for planning correspond to the two you wrote down in question one? Why or why not?

7. During the planning of each of the remembered activities listed above, someone set a goal. Perhaps it was to have a fun party or an interesting trip or for students to learn specific content. In the following space or on a separate piece of paper, set a personal goal for reading this book.

REFERENCES

Ayers, W. (1993). *To teach: The journey of a teacher.* New York: Teachers College Press.

Bean, R., Fulmer, D., Zigmond, N., & Grumet, J. (1995). *How experienced teachers think about their teaching: Their focus, beliefs, and types of reflection.* Paper presented at the meeting of the American Education Research Association, San Francisco, CA.

Brophy, J. (1998). *Motivating students to learn.* Boston, MA: McGraw-Hill.

Burden, P. R., & Byrd, D. M. (2003). *Methods for effective teaching* (3rd ed.). Boston, MA: Pearson Education, Allyn & Bacon.

Clark, C., & Yinger, R. (1979). *Three studies of teacher planning.* East Lansing, MI: Michigan State University, Institute for Research on Teaching.

Council of Chief State School Officers. (1992). *Model standards for beginning teacher licensing and development: A resource for state dialogue [INTASC standards].* Washington, D.C.: Author. http://www.ccsso.org/content/pdfs/corestrd.pdf.

EdSource (2006). *Similar students, different results: Why do some schools do better?* ED491868.

Jones, V. F., & Jones, L. S. (1995). *Comprehensive classroom management: Creating positive learning environments* (4th ed.). Boston, MA: Allyn & Bacon.

Kaestle, C. F. (1983). *Pillars of the republic: Common schools and American society, 1780–1860.* New York: Hill and Wang.

Kauchak, D. P., & Eggen, P. D. (2003). *Learning and teaching: Research-based methods* (4th ed.). Boston, MA: Pearson Education, Allyn & Bacon.

Kintsch, W., & Bates, E. (1977). Recognition memory for statements from a classroom lecture. *Journal of Experimental Psychology: Human Learning and Memory, 3*, 150–159.

McCutcheon, G. (1980). How elementary teachers plan their courses. *Elementary School Journal, 81*, 4–23.

Mintz, A. (1979). *Teacher planning: A simulation study.* Unpublished doctoral dissertation, Syracuse University.

Mondale, S. (2002). *School: The story of American public education.* Boston, MA: Beacon Press.

Morrison, G. S. (2000). *Teaching in America.* Boston, MA: Allyn and Bacon.

Napell, S. (1978). Updating the lecture. *Journal of Teacher Education, 29*(5), 53–56.

National Council for Accreditation of Teacher Education [NCATE]. (2006). *Professional standards for the accreditation of schools, colleges, and departments of education.* Washington, D.C.: Author. Retrieved March, 2007 from http://www.ncate.org/public/standards.asp.

National Council of Teachers of English. (1996). *National standards for the English language arts.* Washington, D.C.: Author (NCTE).

National Research Council. (2000). *How people learn: Brain, mind, experience, and school* (expanded ed.). Washington, D.C.: National Academy Press.

Peterson, P., Marx, R., & Clark, C. (1978). Teacher planning, teacher behavior and student achievement. *American Educational Research Journal, 15*, 417–432.

Roberts, P. L., & Kellough, R. D. (2008). *A guide for developing interdisciplinary thematic units* (3rd ed.). Upper Saddle River, NJ: Merrill/Prentice Hall.

Saurino, D. R., Saurino, P. L., & See, D. (2002). Utilizing visual/spatial techniques and strategies to develop an integrated curriculum: A collaborative group action research approach. Paper presented at the Annual Meeting of the American Educational Research Association. New Orleans, LA (April 1–5, 2002).

Sousa, D. A. (2001). *How the brain learns* (2nd ed.). Thousand Oaks, CA: Corwin Press.

Starko, A. J., Sparks-Langer, G. M., Pasch, M., Frankes, L., Gardner, T. G., & Moody, C. D. (2003). *Teaching as decision making: Successful practices for the elementary teacher* (3rd ed.). Upper Saddle River, NJ: Prentice Hall.

Sullo, R. A. (2007). *Activating the desire to learn.* Alexandria, VA: Association for Supervision and Curriculum Development [ASCD].

U.S. Department of Education. (2003). *Meeting the highly qualified teachers challenge: The Secretary's second annual report on teacher quality, 2003.* Washington, D.C.: Author. Available free at http://www.edpubs.org/webstore/Content/search.asp.

U.S. Department of Education. (2005a). *Education in the United States: A brief overview.* Washington, D.C.: Author. Available free at http://www.edpubs.org/webstore/Content/search.asp.

U.S. Department of Education. (2005b). *Individuals with Disabilities Education Act* (1990, 1997, 2005). Washington, D.C.: Author. Available at http://www.ed.gov.

U.S. Department of Education. (2007). *Building on results: A blueprint for strengthening the "No Child Left Behind Act."* Washington, D.C.: Author. Available free at http://www.ed.gov/policy/elsec/leg/nclb/buildingonresults.html.

Weinstein, C., & Mignano, A. (2007). *Elementary classroom management: Lessons from research and practice* (4th ed.). Boston, MA: McGraw-Hill.

Williams, R., & Ware, J. (1977). An extended visit with Dr. Fox: Validity of student satisfaction with instruction ratings after repeated exposures to a lecturer. *American Educational Research Journal, 14*(4), 449–457.

Zemelman, S., Daniels, H., & Hyde, A. (2005). *Best practice: Today's standards for teaching & learning in America's schools* (3rd ed.). Portsmouth, NH: Heinemann.

Teaching Is Informed Decision Making

Objective: Understand that teachers are informed professional decision makers.

1.1 Make a list of your top three beliefs about learning and teaching.

Relevant INTASC Principles: #1, #2, #3, #4, #5, #6, #7, #8, #9, #10 (See inside back cover of this book for list of INTASC Principles.)

MAKING DECISIONS: EXPERIENCED AND EXPERT TEACHERS

I've come to the frightening conclusion that I am the decisive element in the classroom. It's my personal approach that creates the climate. It's my daily mood that makes the weather. As a teacher, I possess tremendous power to make a child's life miserable or joyous. I can be a tool of torture or an instrument of inspiration. I can humiliate or humor, hurt or heal. In all situations, it is my response that decides whether a crisis will be escalated or de-escalated and a child humanized or de-humanized.

—Haim Ginott

The bell rang. Twenty-some students filed into their math classroom. Music was playing, a popular song; one that the students heard daily on the radio and that most probably had saved on their MP3 players. On their desks, which were shoved against the walls, they found large pieces of colored tagboard with a single numeral printed on each. Instructions on the overhead, which usually contained their problem of the day, told them to pick up their numbers and stand on one of the X's marked on the floor. The music blared away as students slowly began to follow the directions. Once they were all in place they realized they had formed two concentric circles. Suddenly the music stopped and everyone turned toward the silent CD player. Ms. Denton, their math teacher, was standing there.

"I'm going to turn the music back on. When I do, I want everyone in the inner circle to move clockwise. Those of you standing in the outer circle should move counterclockwise. When the music stops, you stop, too. Ready? Move."

The music began and the students began to move, slowly at first. Then some of the "usual suspects" began really moving to the beat. Eventually, everyone was smiling and was feeling less self-conscious. The music stopped.

"Freeze. Face the person to your left who is standing in the other circle. Look at your two numerals. Hold them so that they form an improper fraction. Then hold them together high over your heads. Now!"

Though Ms. Denton's math lesson was not a typical math review, it certainly accomplished what she planned: Students willingly worked together, students were actively engaged in their learning, and she gained information about what her students remembered about proper and improper fractions. There was not a worksheet or quiz in sight. Nor were math books out and about. But certainly, students were "doing math."

Ms. Denton can be described as an informed decision maker. Why? Her curriculum guide listed the study of fractions as required content for her math students. The school provided a class set of fine math textbooks for use by her students, and there was an equally good teacher's edition that provided sample lesson plans and teaching strategies. In fact, Ms. Denton had implemented several of the ideas during the study of fractions. But she didn't just blindly implement a standard curriculum. She wanted to match her instruction to her particular students, their level of readiness, their interests, their learning styles and learning rates. She used ideas from other sources in addition to the teacher's edition as well as knowledge of her students.

She had often heard one of her fellow math teachers say to administrators, "Just tell me what to teach, how to teach it, and when it should be taught. Then leave me alone." In fact, Ms. Denton had seen that teacher's three-inch-thick binder that contained the entire year's lessons; the same ones she had used for the past four years, still unchanged, though the students were certainly different each year. Although Ms. Denton and her colleague have taught for about the same number of years, the colleague could be considered an **experienced teacher,** while Ms. Denton could be called an **expert teacher.**

Although expert and experienced teachers may not differ in the amount of knowledge they have about curriculum or teaching

Reality Check

Question: How do you as an administrator describe expert teachers?

An expert teacher has confidence. . . . Confidence in content, pedagogy, and classroom management. Experience alone doesn't bring this. It is a product of education, training, and reflective practice that informs every decision the teacher makes. These teachers quickly become the "go to" teachers in their buildings and departments, the teacher that principals rely on as well as their sometimes more experienced colleagues.

Dutch Schoenfeldt
Anderson Community Schools

strategies, they do differ in how they organize and use their content knowledge. Experts' knowledge is more integrated. They combine new subject matter content knowledge with students' prior knowledge and make lessons uniquely their own by changing, combining, and adding to them according to their students' needs and their own goals (Hattie, Clinton, Thompson, & Schmitt-Davis, 1996; Posner, 2004).

THE IMPORTANCE OF A PERSONAL PHILOSOPHY OF TEACHING

Philosophy is the theory of education as a deliberately conducted practice.

—John Dewey

Teachers applying for jobs are often asked to explain their personal philosophy of education. Why would a teacher need to articulate a personal philosophy? In his book, *The Skillful Teacher* (2001), Stephen Brookfield points out that the development of a teaching philosophy can provide a clear picture to yourself and others that explains why you are doing what you are doing in your classroom. A personal philosophy, therefore, helps define the reasons for your decisions.

Since the 1970s, educational researchers have examined teachers' beliefs about teaching and learning, and the impact of those beliefs on decision making. Clark and Peterson (1986) refer to it as examining the mental lives of teachers. They suggest that a teacher's mental life is circular or cyclical; a teacher's philosophy (belief system) affects planning and implementation decisions, which in turn shape the teacher's personal philosophy.

What is the connection between a personal philosophy of education and being an informed decision maker? Brubaker and

TECHNOLOGY IN EDUCATION

To view examples of **personal philosophies** of education, go to
http://www.wilderdom.com/philosophy/SampleEducationPhilosophies.html#Links.

Simon (1993) note that "values are at the core of the decision-making process" (p. 12). So that a teacher can feel comfortable with the actions he takes, his decisions must align with his philosophy. Articulation of one's belief system should lead to the confidence to participate actively in the professional decision-making process rather than merely implementing ideas determined by others (Barbour, 1986). This idea relates directly back to the example of Ms. Denton and her colleague at the beginning of this chapter.

PHILOSOPHY: BEST PRACTICE, A K–12 LESSON PLANNING MODEL THAT WORKS

The foundational ideas, concepts, values, and beliefs behind the philosophy used to support the ideas in this book about lesson planning are visually conceptualized in Figure 2.1, and further elaborated in Figure 2.2. In addition, the teacher standards from the Interstate New Teacher Assessment and Support Consortium (INTASC) play an integral part in the philosophy. The INTASC standards, or principles, identify a "common core of teaching knowledge

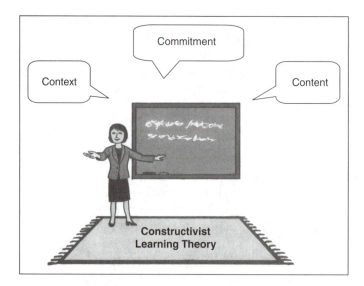

FIGURE 2.1 Constructivist Learning Theory Concepts

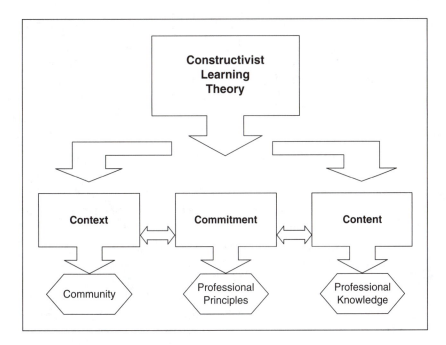

FIGURE 2.2   Constructivist Learning Theory Flowchart

and skills that should be acquired by all new teachers" (Council of Chief State School Officers, 1992, p. 6).

The primary foundational belief concerning teaching and learning presented in this text is that students typically learn best through constructivist pedagogies. **Constructivist pedagogies** allow learners to construct meaning for themselves by making personal connections to new learning and through interactions with others within the educational setting. Behaviorists assert that knowledge is passively absorbed. Cognitive constructivists, including Jean Piaget, reject that idea, arguing instead that knowledge is actively constructed by learners. Behaviorism's focus is on observable behavior. Cognitive constructivism focuses on what goes on "inside the learner's head." Cognitivists encourage strategies that help students to actively engage with new information (Brooks & Brooks, 1993). **Social constructivism** is a variety of cognitive constructivism that emphasizes the collaborative nature of learning. Social constructivists, such as Lev Vygotsky, would encourage the use of such strategies as cooperative groups and other types of peer interaction (Doolittle, 1997).

CONSTRUCTIVISM

Constructing knowledge can occur whether a teacher decides to use more traditional approaches, such as direct instruction and expository teaching, or more indirect instruction such as inquiry learning. As long as the teacher's goal is to actively engage the learners, any instructional approach may be used in a lesson plan. Constructivist learning theory forms the foundation of the philosophy of lesson planning presented in this text.

Context

With feet firmly planted in constructivist theory, the teacher as informed decision maker considers the context, content, and her commitment to professional principles in order to plan effective instruction. **Context,** in this case, refers to *community.* The community contains people, and understanding the needs and expectations of those people is of utmost importance in a teacher's decision-making process. Teachers must consider the *community of learners* in the classroom, their *parents,* and also the *larger community* of which the school and classroom are a part.

Teachers, of course, must consider the students when planning instruction. Content must be subject, grade, and age appropriate. This idea is clearly defined in INTASC Principles 1 and 2: The teacher understands content and how children learn and develop. Teachers must also meet the needs of the various types of learners. Thoughtful consideration must be given to varying learning rates, styles, readiness, and interests. This idea is found in INTASC Principle 3: The teacher understands how students differ in their approaches to learning (Council of Chief State School Officers, 1992).

Parents are a child's first teacher. Parents continue to affect their children's achievement once they start their formal education. Munoz (2000) found that kindergarten children whose parents served as classroom volunteers had increased reading test scores. Simmons-Morton and Crump (2003) found that middle schoolers' adjustment to and engagement in school was closely linked to active parent involvement. High school parent volunteerism is very different from that found in elementary grades. However, research has shown (Fan, 2001) that high school parents who volunteer in extracurricular activities and parent-teacher organizations do continue to have a positive impact on students' academic achievement.

The larger community in which a school is located may be wealthy, middle class, or poor; offer many resources or few; be rural, suburban, or urban. Each of these factors affects the decisions a teacher makes. Each offers different opportunities for school-community partnerships. An expert teacher learns about the community in which she teaches, striving to become an active member. Teachers foster a good working relationship with parents and the larger community, as described in INTASC Principles 7 and 10, so that they can support their students' learning (Council of Chief State School Officers, 1992).

TECHNOLOGY IN EDUCATION

To read more about **constructivist learning theory** go to http://gsi.berkeley.edu/resources/learning/introduction.html or http://www.funderstanding.com/constructivism.cfm.

To see a list of research-based instructional strategies, go to http://www.mcrel.org/Newsroom/hottopicInstruction.asp.

View the **INTASC Principles** online and in more depth at http://www.ccsso.org/content/pdfs/corestrd.pdf.

To view **short videos** that discuss the following **topics,** go to http://www.edutopia.org/. Select Video Library, then Browse Videos by Topic: Emotional Intelligence, Parent Involvement, Community Partnerships.

Commitment

A well-informed teacher must also have a **commitment to** certain **professional principles.** Being a **reflective practitioner** is at the heart of the professional principles (see INTASC Principle 9). Teachers reflect on their decisions in order to continually improve their practice and their students' learning (Council of Chief State School Officers, 1992).

In this text, it is also imperative for the informed decision maker to have *high expectations for all learners,* which includes believing all students can learn. Once that belief becomes part of a philosophy of teaching, a teacher is committed to the idea of *differentiating* instruction, because teachers recognize that students learn in different ways and at different rates. Another core element of believing all children can learn is the desire to select *culturally responsive* materials, making sure materials help all children connect with lesson content. These ideas also contribute to creating a *safe environment;* one that ensures physical safety and also ensures emotional safety, where students will feel free to take risks, share their thoughts, explore creatively, and work collaboratively with others (see INTASC Principles 5, 6, and 7) (Council of Chief State School Officers, 1992).

Content

What factors are at play, for example, when people of high IQ flounder and those of modest IQ do surprisingly well? I would argue that the difference quite often lies in the abilities called emotional intelligence, which include self-control, zeal and persistence, and the ability to motivate oneself.

—Daniel Goleman (2005)

Knowledge of **content** is, of course, key in making informed decisions. Teachers must understand the "what" and the "how" of teaching. **Content knowledge** refers to one's understanding of the subject matter, and **pedagogical knowledge** refers to one's understanding of teaching and learning processes independent of subject matter. **Pedagogical content knowledge** refers to knowledge about the teaching and learning of particular subject matter, taking into account its particular learning demands (Schulman, 1987). The outstanding teacher is not simply a teacher, but rather a math teacher, a reading teacher, or a history teacher. There are generic teaching skills, but many of the pedagogical skills of an outstanding teacher are content-specific. "Beginning teachers need to learn not just 'how to teach,' but rather 'how to teach electricity,' 'how to teach world history,' or 'how to teach fractions'" (Geddis, 1993, p. 575).

Teachers must not only be knowledgeable in academic and pedagogical content, but must be able to make pedagogical decisions that involve the use of a variety of **research-based instructional and assessment strategies** (see INTASC Principles 4, 7, and 8) (Council of Chief State School Officers, 1992). Since the 1970s educational researchers have examined what strategies have a positive impact on student achievement. These include, but are not limited to, one-to-one tutoring, identifying similarities and differences, cooperative learning, nonlinguistic representations, questioning, and using advance organizers.

IN SUMMARY

Teachers are professionals. They must become informed decision makers. They should have enthusiasm for teaching and be committed to the idea that all decisions and the subsequent actions must be in the best interest of their students. Effective teachers are active decision makers who have the knowledge and self-confidence to create meaningful learning experiences for their students, rather than merely individuals who implement a prescribed curriculum and decisions made by others.

YOUR TURN

 ACTIVITY 1: Your Beliefs

INTASC Principle 9

Directions: Answer the following questions.

1. What are the purposes of public education?

2. What is the teacher's role?

 ACTIVITY 2: Your Philosophy

INTASC Principle 9

Directions: Answer the following question.

1. List your top three beliefs about teaching and learning.

   a.

   b.

   c.

 ACTIVITY 3: Reflection

INTASC Principles 9 and 10

Directions: Answer the following questions.

1. How will your beliefs influence your professional decision making?

2. What will you do or not do because of what you believe?

3. Discuss your ideas with two other people who are reading this book. How are your beliefs similar and different?

REFERENCES

Barbour, N. (1986, May/June). Teachers can make decisions. *Childhood Education,* 322–324.

Brookfield, S. D. (2001). *The skillful teacher.* Hoboken, NJ: Wiley.

Brooks, J., & Brooks, M. (1993). *In search of understanding: The case for constructivist classrooms.* Alexandria, VA: Association for Supervision and Curriculum Development.

Brubaker, D. L., & Simon, L. H. (1993). *Teacher as decision-maker.* Newbury Park, CA: Sage.

Clark, C. M., & Peterson, P. L. (1986). Teachers' thought processes. In M. C. Witrock (Ed.), *Handbook of research on teaching.* New York: Macmillan.

Council of Chief State School Officers. (1992). *Model standards for beginning teacher licensing and development: A resource for state dialogue [INTASC standards].* Washington, D.C.: Author. Retrieved from http://www.ccsso.org/content/pdfs/corestrd.pdf.

Doolittle, P. E. (1997). Vygotsky's zone of proximal development as a theoretical foundation for cooperation learning. *Journal on Excellence in College Teaching, 8*(1), 83–103.

Fan, X. (2001). Parental involvement and students' academic achievement: A growth modeling analysis. *Journal of Experimental Education, 70*(1), 27–53.

Geddis, A. N. (1993). Transforming content knowledge: Learning to teach about isotopes. *Science Education, 77,* 575–591.

Goleman, D. (2005). *Emotional intelligence* (10th anniversary ed.). New York: Bantam.

Hattie, J. A., Clinton, J. C., Thompson, M., & Schmitt-Davis, H. (1996). *Identifying expert teachers.* Chapel Hill, NC: North Carolina Association for Research in Education.

Munoz, M. A. (2000). *Parental volunteerism in kindergarten: Assessing its impact in reading and mathematics test.* (Report No. PS030368). University of Louisville, KY. (ERIC Document Reproduction Service No. ED464745).

Posner, G. J. (2004). *Analyzing the curriculum* (3rd ed.). Boston: McGraw-Hill.

Schulman, L. S. (1987). Knowledge and teaching: Foundations of the New Reform. *Harvard Educational Review, 57*(1), 1–22.

Simmons-Morton, G., & Crump, A. D. (2003). Association of parental involvement and social competence with school adjustment and engagement among sixth graders. *Journal of School Health, 73*(3), 121–126.

PART II

Structural Foundations of a Lesson Plan

3

Identifying a Topic
and Academic Standards

Objective: Connect a selected topic to academic content standards.

1.1 Select a topic of instruction.

1.2 Select relevant academic standards from at least one subject area.

Using our road trip analogy, identifying a topic is deciding on what type of trip to take: a trip to the mountains, the beach, or to a big city. Then we can use the map to see where we might want to go and how to get there (Figure 3.1, p. 34).

Relevant INTASC Principles: #1, #6, #7, #9 (See inside back cover.)

IDENTIFYING TOPICS

The first step in planning a lesson is to identify the topic you plan to teach. Deciding on the type of trip to take is analogous to selecting a topic. You could get in your car one day and begin to drive without any clear idea of where you are going. Although it may be exciting not to know your destination when you begin the trip, you might find yourself in the middle of nowhere with nothing to see or do. It would have been more useful to ask the following questions before setting out on an adventure: Where do we want to go, mountains, beach, big city? What interests us, skiing, surfing and swimming, shopping?

A **topic** is any theme, issue (question), or problem that can be the main idea of the lesson. Research studies indicate that planning most commonly begins with a topic. Teachers identify a lesson plan topic as they consider which content is important for students to learn. Lesson plan topics come from organized collections of

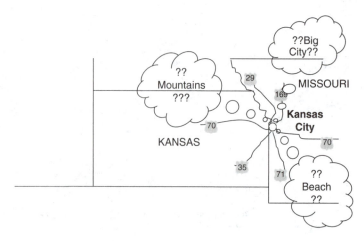

FIGURE 3.1   Choosing a Road Trip Destination

knowledge "that combine facts, concepts, generalizations, and the relationships among them" (Kauchak & Eggen, 2003, p. 210).

Teachers can find topics in several locations. Most likely they choose a topic from their school district or school's curricular program or textbooks, within the district or school's scope and sequence for subject areas; or topics developed by members of a grade level or subject teaching team. There are many different definitions of curriculum, but broadly speaking, the term **curriculum** refers to the content to be taught (Burden & Byrd, 2003; Morrison, 2000; Posner, 1995).

School districts purchase curriculum from vendors (e.g., textbooks and kits), hire personnel such as curriculum specialists to write curriculum, encourage teachers to write their own curriculum, or combine all of these to meet the curricular needs at each grade level. Topics in textbooks and curriculum programs can change from year to year (Kellough & Roberts, 2002). Therefore, teachers adjust their lesson topics to those designated in the curriculum or textbooks (Woodward & Elliott, 1990).

 ## Reality Check

Question: How do you decide what topics to teach?

I decide on topics according to what the state of Arizona deems necessary to teach for my grade level, and I look at the district's Scope and Sequence. I also look at my particular group of students. I have taught for over 30 years in a predominantly lower socioeconomic area. So more than anything I based my topics on the students' prior knowledge, or lack of, and then went to the Scope and Sequence and state standards.

Barbara Martin
Sixth-grade social studies
Arizona

Topics may also come from the interests of students or teachers themselves. Those topics selected by students, or based on their interests, provide motivating learning opportunities. Students respond more actively to topics that are related to their interests, which in turn may stimulate teachers to plan interactive and challenging lessons (Ausubel, 1977). In the road trip analogy, the topic is determining what type of trip we want to take. We could go to a beach, to the mountains, or to a large city. Our interests will help us decide. We don't want a crowded, noisy city and we don't like sand, so we decide to go to the mountains.

IDENTIFYING ACADEMIC STANDARDS

Many factors affect the success of a trip. After we have decided on the type of trip, we consult a road map to help us find options. We decide to choose a trip to the mountains in Utah, Colorado, or Vermont. The success of a lesson plan, student learning, depends on the decisions the teacher makes as it is written.

The lesson planning process is influenced by national, state, and local academic content standards. The standards provide a road map for teachers as they plan short-term and long-term learning experiences. **Standards** are statements that describe the subject matter students should know and perform at each grade level (Eggen & Kauchak, 2006). The U.S. Department of Education (2006) provides the following definition of content standards:

> *Content standards* are broad descriptions of the knowledge and skills students should acquire in the core academic subjects. The knowledge includes the important and enduring ideas, concepts, issues, and information of the subject areas. The skills include the ways of thinking, working, communicating, reasoning, and investigating that characterize each subject area. Content standards may emphasize interdisciplinary themes as well as concepts in the core academic subjects. (p. 3)

STANDARDS AND EDUCATIONAL REFORM

In 1983 the National Commission on Excellence in Education published a report titled *A Nation at Risk* (Burden & Byrd, 2003). The report provided recommendations to improve the quality of education in the United States. The recommendations stressed the need for increased classroom instruction on the basics of education, more stringent graduation requirements, accountability through standards-based tests, and development of academic standards.

A national education review began at the Charlottesville Education Summit in 1989 to consider possible accountability measures for increasing students' achievement and promoting higher expectations of curriculum and instruction in the classroom. Following the summit, the National Association of Governors and the president of the United States agreed on the following six broad national goals for education:

The National Education Goals

Goal 1: By the year 2000, all children in America will start school ready to learn.

Goal 2: By the year 2000, the high school graduation rate will increase to at least 90 percent.

Goal 3: By the year 2000, American students will leave grades four, eight, and twelve having demonstrated competency in challenging subject matter, including English, mathematics, science, history, and geography; and every school in America will ensure that all students learn to use their minds well, so they may be prepared for responsible citizenship, further learning, and productive employment in our modern economy.

Goal 4: By the year 2000, U.S. students will be first in the world in science and mathematics achievement.

Goal 5: By the year 2000, every adult American will be literate and will possess the knowledge and skills necessary to compete in a global economy and exercise the rights and responsibilities of citizenship.

Goal 6: By the year 2000, every school in America will be free of drugs and violence and will offer a disciplined environment conducive to learning. (The National Education Goals Panel, 1993, pp. 2–4)

The bipartisan and intergovernmental panel of federal and state officials met again in July 1990 to assess and report state and national progress toward achieving the National Education Goals.

In 1994, the Goals 2000: Educate America Act became a law intended to energize public opinion and mandate ongoing education reform through accountability efforts and higher expectations for all students, the schools, and other learning systems (The National Education Goals Panel, 1993). The development of a comprehensive plan for educating America's youth has had a great impact on the way children are taught throughout the nation. The national subject area education organizations began developing content area goals for K–12 subject matter content.

NATIONAL STANDARDS

The goals became academic standards, developed first for mathematics, English language arts, geography, social studies, and science. These standards were created and published during a period of time in the 1990s that has been dubbed "The Standards Movement." These standards were developed by national organizations: the National Council of Teachers of Mathematics in 1991 (NCTM, 2000), the Standards Project for the

TECHNOLOGY IN EDUCATION

Go to http://www.socialstudies.org/standards/strands/. Look at the organization of the National Social Studies Standards.

Use a search engine, like Google, to find the National Science Standards. Is their organization similar to the social studies standards?

Find your state's academic standards. Examine the science standards. Is their organization similar to that of the national standards?

English Language Arts in 1992 (NCTE, 2006), the Geography Education Standards Project in 1994, the National Council for the Social Studies in 1994, and the National Science Teachers Association in 1996. Facts, concepts, skills, and principles from each subject area were identified for students at each grade level.

One example of a subject area that includes multiple disciplines is social studies. The integrated areas of the social sciences, behavioral sciences, and humanities are subsumed within the social studies curriculum. The National Council for the Social Studies (1994, p. 3) defines social studies curriculum as a "coordinated, systematic study drawing upon such disciplines as anthropology, archaeology, economics, geography, history, law, philosophy, political science, psychology, religion, and sociology."

Language arts curriculum is another subject area that encapsulates multiple discipline areas. Language arts address the fundamental skills of reading, writing, listening, and speaking. The California Reading Task Force (1995) developed an example of a comprehensive and balanced program for language arts. The state's approach to reading must contain:

(1) a strong literature, language, and comprehension program that includes a balance of written language; (2) an organized, explicit skills program that includes phonemic awareness (sounds in words), phonics, and decoding skills to address the needs of the emergent reader; (3) ongoing diagnosis that informs teaching and assessment that ensures accountability; and (4) a powerful early intervention program that provides individual tutoring for students at risk of failure in reading. (California Reading Task Force, 1995, p. 19)

STATE STANDARDS

Each state has developed its own state academic standards. Most can be found at that state's Department of Education's Web site or by using a search engine to find a separate Web site dedicated to the state's standards. The states do not all use the same terminology to describe the various components of their standards. One state may use the term *benchmark* to describe specific content to be learned. Another state may use the term *standard indicators* to identify or name similar ideas.

Some state standards are written as broad, generalized statements, while others are precisely written, clearly identifying specific concepts and processes. In the Texas Essential Knowledge and Skills (TEKS), the learning standards for children attending school in the state of Texas, there are both types of standards. A broadly written second-grade TEKS English language arts and reading standard example asks students to "listen responsively to stories and other texts read aloud." An example of a more precisely worded standard is the second-grade TEKS mathematics standard that states students will "read a thermometer to gather data" (Texas Education Agency, 2001).

Broadly written standards may relate to several lesson topics, as the language arts example above shows, because teachers read many books, poems, and plays aloud to their students over the course of a year. The sample mathematics standard, more narrowly focused, gives more precise direction for the lesson planner.

When planning a lesson, teachers first select a topic. This topic is usually found in the local school curriculum or textbooks. The next decision is to find relevant academic standards that will help the teacher identify specific knowledge, skills, and concepts of the given topic.

IDENTIFY A TOPIC AND STANDARDS FOR A LESSON

Teachers organize their lessons, and units, around the body of knowledge of a selected topic as defined in academic standards. The facts, concepts, processes, generalizations, and relationships between them form the focus for each lesson. One teacher may

 Reality Check

Question: How do you decide what topics and standards to teach?

I decide what to teach by looking at state standards and textbooks that are used in our district. . . . I have taught long enough (in my state) and am very familiar with standards at my grade level; I know what is relevant and plan accordingly, making sure we cover all important information for testing.

Linda Williams
Quail Run Elementary
Fourth grade

Reality Check

Question: How do you incorporate standards in your lesson plans?

I have recently learned in my graduate education courses about the Understanding by Design process, which urges teachers to do lesson planning "backwards"—beginning with the standards and planning the lesson around them. I believe this is a practical and constructive way to plan lessons.

Sarah Miller
First/second grade Kapolei Elementary
Hawaii

read the school district's curricular guide and then identify a standard from one subject area. Another teacher may select a topic the students find interesting, then search for associated standards from a variety of disciplines. Each option requires a teacher to analyze the topic to determine which content-related facts, concepts, and principles should be taught during the lesson as outlined by the standard (Lang & Evans, 2006).

Ms. Jones has selected the topic of insects for her third-grade classroom. She found the topic in her district's curriculum guide for third grade. Then she consulted her state's science standards and found Science Standard 4: The Living Environment matched with her topic. She skimmed down through the benchmark statements and found one that mentioned that third graders should learn that living things can be sorted into groups. This gave Ms. Jones the idea to teach the children about the parts of an insect and how insects differ from other groups of animals like mammals and birds.

Ms. Smith selected the topic of insects for her third-grade classroom, too. Besides identifying the same science standard and benchmark statement, Ms. Smith looked at the social studies standard for geography and found a benchmark statement about identifying local environmental issues and ways that have been used to solve problems. Ms. Smith knows that her community is in an agricultural region and knows that insects can be both helpful and harmful to farmers. She decides to add this to her lesson on insects because many of her students live on farms.

Mr. Johnson, a high school science teacher, planned a lesson to help his students better understand the topic of the universe. He chose a standard that required students to research how manned and unmanned space vehicles increase our knowledge of the universe. Mr. Morton, in the same high school, chose a different standard that emphasized having students compare the size, temperature, and age of the planets in our universe. These two examples demonstrate that the selection of standards affects the direction lessons based on the same topic can take.

It may be necessary for a teacher to conduct a needs assessment or task analysis to identify students' learning needs after identifying the topic and standard. A **needs assessment** is a tool for determining whether there is a need for instruction and intervention (Kemp, Morrison, & Ross, 1994). Pretests, K-W-L charts, and brainstorming are a few methods of determining the prior knowledge students already possess of the topic. If the students already know the content, then a short review, rather than an entire lesson dedicated to the content may suffice. Or perhaps the children know very little about the topic, and so the teacher will plan experiences with the topic prior to the lesson. If the topic selected is the rainforest, and in a prelesson discussion the teacher finds out that the children are unfamiliar with the term, she may decide to create interest and some prior knowledge experiences for her students. She can do so by decorating a bulletin board that shows photos taken in a rainforest, placing books at the reading center about animals and plants found in a rainforest, and reading a story that takes place in a rainforest. Then when she begins her lesson on the rainforest, the children will have some prior knowledge of the topic.

Task analysis is when a topic is broken into portions, which are then analyzed for the content information students must acquire. Smith and Ragan (2005) suggest "prerequisite skills may be confirmed by testing groups of learners who do and do not possess the targeted skills" (p. 328). If some students know the prerequisite content well and others do not, then the teacher may divide the students into small groups for instruction; each group works on the part of the content that they are ready to learn. If the topic is, for example, writing four-line poems with an "aa bb" rhyming pattern, and some children are still struggling with rhyming words, then the teacher can help those children work with rhyming words while other children begin writing two lines that rhyme.

IN SUMMARY

The first step in writing a lesson plan is to identify a topic. Most teachers find the topics in their school curriculum guides or in textbooks. The next step is to use academic standards to identify relevant content for the selected topic. Sometimes these standards are already listed in the district's curriculum. However, since that is not always the case, it is important for teachers to know how to incorporate standards themselves.

UNIT CONNECTION

"Real life" is not segmented into subject areas. This is the idea behind creating interdisciplinary units of study. A unit of instruction is a series of lessons connected by their topic.

Unit planning requires the selection of content-related concepts, skills, and perspectives from multiple subject areas. Teachers select one broad topic or theme, such as tornadoes, as the focal point for a unit of study. Then they search for standards from more than one subject area so that students study the topic from multiple perspectives.

In a tornadoes unit, students could study how tornadoes form in science; map the location of Tornado Alley in social studies; read and write stories about tornadoes in language arts; and in health, learn what to do in case a tornado strikes. Finding the relevant standards helps the teacher further identify specific skills and knowledge to include in each lesson.

 # YOUR TURN

 ### ACTIVITY 1: Your State Standards

INTASC Principles 1, 9, and 10

Directions: Answer the following questions.

1. Find and list the URL for the Web site for your state's academic standards. You may want to bookmark it on your computer.
2. Are your state's standards generally stated, very specific, or a mixture of both?
3. Does your state use the term *benchmark*? If so, to what does it refer? List a sample benchmark statement.

   OR

3. Does your state use the term *standard indicator*? If so, to what does it refer? List a sample standard indicator.

 # TECHNOLOGY IN EDUCATION

Check the following Web site for topic ideas. You can search by subject/discipline area along the right-hand side of the home page: http://www.thinkfinity.org/.

Or try this Web site: http://www.earthwatch.org/site/.

Or use a search engine to look for topics. Use *lesson plan topics* as your search term.

ACTIVITY 2: Topic Identification

INTASC Principles 1, 2, and 7

Directions:

Some basic discipline areas are listed here. In a small group, generate a list of two or more topics related to each of the subject areas. You may use grade-level textbooks or a school's curriculum guide for ideas. You may also search online teacher sites for topic ideas.

1. Social studies:

2. Science:

3. Mathematics:

4. Language arts:

 ACTIVITY 3: Select and Align a Topic with State Academic Standards

INTASC Principles 1, 2, and 7

Directions:

1. Choose a topic for the lesson plan you will be creating. Decide with which content area your topic most closely aligns (science, social studies, etc.).

   Topic:

   Content area:

2. Select a grade level:

3. Go to the Internet bookmark of your state's curricular standards.

4. Identify one or more state standards to guide you in developing the topic.

   Standard:

   Standard: (optional)

 ACTIVITY 4: Reflection

INTASC Principle 9

Directions: Answer the following questions.

1. How will you know what curriculum to teach?

2. How does deciding on a topic affect lesson planning?

3. What role do state academic standards play in creating a lesson plan?

REFERENCES

Ausubel, D. (1977). The facilitation of meaningful verbal learning in the classroom. *Educational Psychologist, 12*(2), 162–178.

Burden, P. R., & Byrd, D. M. (2003). *Methods for effective teaching* (3rd ed.). Boston: Pearson Education, Allyn & Bacon.

California Reading Task Force. (1995). Goal and key components of effective language arts instruction [Draft only]. Retrieved June 1, 2006, from http://www.cde.ca.gov/ci/rl/cf.

Eggen, P. D., & Kauchak, D. P. (2006). *Strategies and models for teachers: Teaching content and thinking skills* (5th ed.). Boston: Pearson Education.

Geography Education Standards Project. (1994). *Geography for life: National Geography Standards.* Washington, D.C.: American Geographical Society, Association of American Geographers, National Council for Geographic Education, and National Geographic Society.

Kauchak, D. P., & Eggen, P. D. (2003). *Learning and teaching: Research-based methods* (4th ed.). Boston: Pearson Education, Allyn & Bacon.

Kellough, R. D., & Roberts, P. L. (2002). *A resource guide for elementary school teaching: Planning for competence* (5th ed.). Upper Saddle River, NJ: Merrill Prentice Hall.

Kemp, J. E., Morrison, G. R., & Ross, S. M. (1994). *Designing effective instruction.* New York: Macmillan College.

Lang, H. R., & Evans, D. N. (2006). *Models, strategies, and methods for effective teaching.* Boston: Pearson Education.

Morrison, G. S. (2000). *Teaching in America* (2nd ed.). Needham Heights, MA: Allyn & Bacon, Pearson Education.

National Council of Teachers of English & International Reading Association. (2006). *Standards for the English language arts.* Urbana, IL: National Council of Teachers of English. Retrieved May 29, 2006, from http://www.ncte.org/about/over/standards/110846.htm.

National Council of Teachers of Mathematics (2000). *NCTM unveiled updated mathematics standards: Marks the compilation of lessons learned over the last ten years.* Retrieved May 29, 2006, from http://www.nctm.org/standards/pressrelease. htm.

National Council for the Social Studies. (1994). *Expectations of excellence: Curriculum standards for social studies.* Washington, D.C.: National Council for the Social Studies.

The National Education Goals Panel. (1993). *The National Education Goals Report.* Retrieved April 25, 2006, from http://www.ed.gov/pubs/goals/report/goalsrpt.txt.

National Science Teachers Association. (1996). *National science education standards.* Retrieved June 1, 2006, from http://www.nsta.org/standards.

Posner, G. J. (1995). *Analyzing the curriculum* (2nd ed.). New York: McGraw-Hill.

Smith, P. L., & Ragan, T. J. (2005). *Instructional design* (3rd ed.). Hoboken, NJ: Wiley–Jossey-Bass Education.

Texas Education Agency. (2001). *Texas essential knowledge and skills (TEKS): Learning standards for Texas children (A summary for parents).* Texas Education Agency. Retrieved April 26, 2006, from http://www.tea.state.tx.us/teks/index.html.

U.S. Department of Education. (2006). *Guidance on standards, assessments, and accountability: Content and performance standards questions and answers* [Archived information]. Retrieved April 24, 2006, from http://www.ed.gov/policy/elsec/guid/standardsassessment/ guidance_pg3.html#introduction2.

Woodward, A., & Elliott, D. L. (Ed.). (1990). Textbooks: Consensus and controversy (Chap. 10). In *Textbooks and schooling in the United States: Eighty-ninth yearbook of the National Society for the Study of Education*, Part I. Chicago: National Society for the Study of Education [NSSE].

Writing Lesson Goals and Objectives

Objective: Plan for instruction.

1.1 Write one lesson goal.

1.2 Write one lesson objective.

Using our road trip analogy, a goal is deciding what type of trip to take and the lesson objective is the specific destination. We decided to take a trip to the mountains (topic) and used a map (standards) to help us see that we had options of places to go for a trip to the mountains: Colorado, Vermont, Utah. Now, we decide our goal is to go skiing and our objective is to ski in the Denver, Colorado, area (Figure 4.1, p. 46).

Relevant INTASC Principles: #1, #2, #3, #4, #5, #6, #7, #8, #9 (See inside back cover.)

> *A goal without a plan is just a wish.*
>
> —Antoine de Saint-Exupéry

GOALS AND OBJECTIVES

Purpose for Writing Goals and Objectives

The main reason to write goals and objectives is to *communicate.* Goals and objectives help *clarify the intent of instruction* and help in *defining expectations of students.* Clearly articulated goals and objectives communicate intent to all stakeholders of the educational process: the teacher, students, parents, school administrators, school board members, and the community. Clarifying the intended learning outcomes provides a foundation for lesson and unit planning, and guides in assessment development and selection of teaching materials and methods.

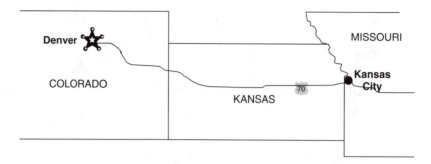

FIGURE 4.1 Deciding on the Road Trip's Type and Locations

To communicate effectively, a teacher must have a clear idea of the intended results of instruction. A favorite phrase to describe objective writing is, "Begin with the end in mind." Without a clear idea of what he wishes students to know or be able to do after instruction, it is difficult for a teacher to write an objective. Without an objective, it is nearly impossible to write a lesson plan that will lead to meaningful student learning.

> *For the want of a nail, the shoe was lost; for the want of a shoe the horse was lost; and for the want of a horse the rider was lost, being overtaken and slain by the enemy, all for the want of care about a horseshoe nail.*
>
> —Benjamin Franklin

To paraphrase Franklin:

For the want of a goal, the objective was lost; for the want of an objective, the lesson was lost; and for the want of a lesson, the student was lost, being overtaken by ignorance, all for the want of care about the lesson goal.

Defining Goals and Objectives

Often the terms *goals* and *objectives* are used interchangeably, but they have different meanings. Although each term is used to identify an expected outcome or state instructional intent, a **goal** is a broad, general statement about the expected outcome of a lesson or series of lessons. Examples of goals:

- Become a better writer.
- Improve hand-eye coordination.
- Learn to use metric measurements.
- Use a variety of reference materials.
- Understand basic economic terms.
- Define ideas related to circles.
- Design an original work of art.

These goals are not specific enough to use to teach a lesson. Teachers, having a goal or end result of learning in mind, then develop lesson objectives. An **objective** is a specific statement of a learning outcome. Examples of objectives:

- Write a topic sentence.
- Dribble a basketball.
- Measure and record the length of the classroom to the nearest meter.
- Use a thesaurus to create a list of synonyms for a given word.
- Create lists of goods and services provided in the local community.
- Find the center of a circle by drawing the perpendicular bisector of two chords.
- Identify the function and meaning of symbols used in an original piece of artwork.

Academic standards are often arranged into goals and objectives. For example, Indiana academic Mathematics Standard 5: Measurement for second grade: "Understand how to measure length, temperature, capacity, weight, and time in standard units." Indiana academic Mathematics Standard 5: Standard Indicator 2.5.1: "Measure and estimate length to the nearest meter" (Indiana Department of Education, 2004).

It is easy to see that Standard 5 is a broad, general statement of what students are expected to learn. They are to learn to measure using standard units. This is a goal. The standard indicator (2.5.1) is much more specific. Now it is clear that the students are to measure using meters. This is an objective.`

In our road trip analogy, we needed to decide the reason for going to the mountains. We could go hiking, skiing, fishing, camping, or sightseeing. Once we decided on the goal of skiing, the next decision was to decide specifically where to go skiing. We have previously (1) decided to go to the mountains (topic), (2) chose Colorado using a

Reality Check

Question: Why write goals and objectives?

I usually don't write very detailed lesson plans as I did in college. However, I do put the objectives in my lesson plans. That way I can glance at my lesson plans each morning and see what the main things are I need to teach for the day. They are a quick way for me to do a self-check on my teaching for the day. I can also look at them at the end of the day and see if I covered what I planned to cover.

Matthew A. Huber
Albany Elementary School
First grade

map (standards), (3) decided on a ski vacation (goal), and (4) now we've decided on Denver, a specific place (objective) in Colorado.

APPROACHES TO WRITING LESSON OBJECTIVES

The use of goals and objectives as the starting point for instructional planning began in the late 1940s as a result of Ralph Tyler's text, *Basic Principles of Curriculum and Instruction* (1949). Tyler suggested that teachers should state objectives in terms of (1) what kind of student behavior is to be developed, and (2) the "content or area of life in which this behavior is to operate" (p. 46). This method of writing objectives was largely supplanted by Robert Mager's suggestions for objective writing.

Behavioral Objectives

Robert Mager published *Preparing Instructional Objectives* in 1962. He focused teachers' attention on concrete, observable student outcomes or behaviors. Mager identified three necessary parts to an objective: (1) the conditions in which the behavior will occur, (2) an observable behavior, and (3) the criteria for acceptable performance. Mager's objectives are called **behavioral objectives.** From a behaviorist perspective, the point of education is for teachers to teach students the appropriate behavioral responses to specific stimuli (Skinner, 1976). Behavioral objectives are very specific and are designed to produce observable behaviors or responses to teacher actions or stimuli.

Sample Behavioral Objectives

1. Given 5 sentences, fifth graders will identify each that contains a simile with at least 80% accuracy.
2. Given 10 addition problems requiring regrouping, second graders will successfully solve 8.

Examining Behavioral Objective 1:

Condition: Given 5 sentences

In other words, students will not look in a newspaper or magazine for examples of sentences that contain similes, or be asked to write their own. The teacher will provide the sentences for the students to examine.

Observable behavior: Identify

The observable behavior in a behavioral objective is always stated as an action verb. In this case, students will identify which of the 5 sentences contain a simile. In directions to the students, the teacher will indicate specifically how the student will *identify*. Perhaps the student will be asked to put a checkmark in front of each sentence that contains a simile, or to underline the simile. But the expected behavior that is observable is to identify.

Criteria for acceptable performance: At least 80% accuracy

Students are expected to get at least 4 of the sentences (.80 × 5 = 4) correct.

Goals Objectives

An alternative to Mager's objectives is called the Goals Approach to Preparing Objectives, or simply, goals objectives. A **goals objective** is a statement that answers two teacher questions: (1) What do I want the learner to know, understand, or appreciate? (2) How will I know if the student knows, understands, or appreciates (Jacobsen, Eggen, & Kauchak, 2002)? Goals objectives begin with a general goal statement such as, "Kindergartners should know basic colors." This general statement can answer the first of the two teacher questions, "What do I want the student to know, understand, or appreciate?"

The next part of a goals objective is the evaluation statement that spells out (1) the expected student performance, (2) the conditions under which the student will perform, and (3) the acceptable level of performance. This part of the goals objective answers the second teacher question, "How will I know the student knows, understands, or appreciates?"

A Sample Goals Objective

Kindergartners will know basic colors, so that when shown 6 colored items, they will orally name the color of each correctly.

Examining a Goals Objective:

General goal statement: Kindergartners will know basic colors

Evaluation statement elements:

Expected student performance: Orally name (say aloud) the color's name

Conditions: When shown 6 colored items

Level of performance: 100% accuracy (*correctly* name each)

In the mid-20th century, a different view of learning, called constructivism, emerged. Constructivists believe that learners construct their own understanding of the world through reflecting on experiences and making connections between new information and past experiences. With this shift in the view of how learning takes place came a shift in the way objectives are written.

Instructional Objectives

In 2004 Norman Gronlund, in his book *Writing Instructional Objectives for Teaching and Assessment,* suggested yet another way to write objectives. Gronlund called them **instructional objectives,** and suggested that objectives should first be stated in general terms. This is similar to the goals objectives. A major difference from the goals objectives, however, is that Gronlund believes that setting conditions and criteria are too specific and limit teacher and student flexibility. Instead, he suggests that specific behaviors providing evidence that the learner has met the lesson's objective should follow the general statement. This differs from Mager's objectives in that Gronlund's objectives specify evidence of learning but do not include the intent.

In the book, *Classroom Instruction That Works: Research-Based Strategies for Increasing Student Achievement,* Marzano, Pickering, and Pollock (2001) provide three generalizations about instructional goal setting based on their meta-analysis of studies that examined teacher goal-setting. The first, "instructional goals narrow what students focus on" (p. 94), seems at first reading to be desirable. However, setting an overly specific goal can have the unintended consequence of focusing students' attention so narrowly that they may ignore information that is not specifically related to the learning outcome.

Marzano et al. (2001) also generalize that instructional goals should not be too specific. "Instructional objectives generated using Mager's criteria are obviously highly specific in nature. Perhaps they are simply too specific to accommodate the individual and constructivist nature of the learning process" (p. 94). And third, Marzano et al. (2001) deduced from their research that students should be encouraged to personalize the teacher's goals.

Gronlund's approach is probably the most popular one used among curriculum writers today. His instructional objectives are broader and more inclusive than other approaches. "Course content requiring literally thousands of objectives . . . [using] Mager's approach would be reduced to fewer than one hundred using Gronlund's" approach (Jacobsen et al., 2002, p. 76). Gronlund advocates writing instructional objectives that (1) state general intended learning outcomes that are more specifically defined by (2) listing sample types of student performance. These specific types of performance use action verbs that represent observable student responses. Note that the phrase "Students will" is not used to begin the objective.

Sample Instructional Objective

1. Comprehend basic scientific concepts.

   Define biodegradable.
   Categorize items as biodegradable or nonbiodegradable.

Most general statements in instructional objectives use verbs such as *use, comprehend,* and *know.* The student performance statements use more specific action verbs such as *identify, list, predict, write,* and *interpret* that result in observable student responses. Terms such as *learn, develop an appreciation for, understand,* and *realize* are too general to be used in performance statements and are common mistakes teachers make when trying to write performance statements. Remember that the performance statements use specific action verbs that are directly observable; you, the teacher, see the students doing the action.

The Bloom's Taxonomy chart in Figure 4.2 (p. 52) was adapted to provide a list of verbs that can be used to create objectives that describe observable responses. The original, complete Taxonomy (Bloom, Engelhart, Furst, Hill, & Krathwohl, 1956) defines expectations for three domains of learning: cognitive, affective, and psychomotor. The cognitive domain is concerned with intellectual outcomes and ranges from lower level knowledge to higher levels of thinking that involve synthesis and evaluation. The affective domain is concerned with interests, attitudes, and appreciation, while the psychomotor domain is concerned with motor skills. This Taxonomy can serve as a guide while you learn to write objectives.

STANDARDS-BASED LESSONS: USING ACADEMIC STANDARDS TO WRITE OBJECTIVES

Accountability has become the centerpiece of educational debate and policy development in the United States in recent years. Parents, communities, and state and national legislators are placing new demands for accountability on schools and teachers. In part, this emphasis on accountability led to the development of national academic standards at all grade levels. States, too, have developed standards to describe the academic performance expected of K–12 students in each subject area. It is important, then, that instruction and assessments are all aligned with the appropriate academic standards. Refer to the TiE box for a list of some national subject area professional organizations responsible for writing the standards. The standards can be found on their Web sites.

Most standards provide general statements that teachers can use to form goals. The standards also contain more specific statements that teachers can use to write objectives. These more

Level	Explanation	Sample Verbs
Knowledge	Recall information *Remember*	define identify label match tell list name
Comprehension	Understand meaning *Understand*	describe estimate explain give examples paraphrase rewrite
Application	Use information *Use*	calculate demonstrate illustrate map measure solve
Analysis	See patterns, organize parts *Take Apart*	categorize classify compare diagram examine test for contrast
Synthesis	Generalize from given facts, use information in a new way *Combine in a New Way*	compose construct create design invent modify plan
Evaluation	Make judgments, discriminate between ideas, make choices *Judge*	convince critique defend evaluate interpret judge justify support

Adapted by M. K. Schoenfeldt (2006).

FIGURE 4.2 Bloom's Taxonomy of the Cognitive Domain

 **TECHNOLOGY IN EDUCATION**

Following is a sample list of national subject area organizations and their Web addresses.

ORGANIZATION	STANDARDS TITLE	WEB ADDRESS
National Council for the Social Studies	*Expectations of Experience: Curriculum Standards for Social Studies*	http://www.socialstudies.org/standards/
National Council of Teachers of Mathematics	*Curriculum and Evaluation Standards for School Mathematics*	http://standards.nctm.org/
National Council of Teachers of English and the International Reading Association	*Standards for the English Language Arts*	http://www.readwritethink.org/standards/
National Research Council	*National Science Education Standards*	http://www.nsta.org/

specific statements are sometimes called *benchmarks* or *standard indicators.*

> **Standard 2:** The student understands the interactions of people and the physical environment
>
> **Benchmark statement:** Understands how human activity affects the physical environment (Florida Department of Education, 2005)

This standard explains that elementary students should understand how humans affect the environment. This statement is still too general to serve as an objective. However, the standard can be used as a goal statement. To arrive at one or more examples of specific student responses, it is necessary to make some decisions. It is necessary to determine what students should be able to do with any information they acquire as a result of the lesson. If this is the first time the students will be looking at human impact on the environment, then perhaps they should demonstrate their ability to understand and apply what they have learned. So the Taxonomy verbs for the application level can serve as a guide. Here are some possible objectives for our selected standard at the application level:

Understand the interactions of people and the physical environment.
    1.1 *Give examples* of man-made and naturally occurring objects on the school campus.
    1.2 *Map* the school campus, identifying your examples.

In 1.1, "give examples" is taken from the comprehension level of the Taxonomy; "map," in 1.2, is taken from the application level. Both are examples of observable student response to learning. If the students have worked with this standard before, then it is advisable to write objectives that encourage the higher levels of thinking. Generally, teachers can assume that students must have basic knowledge and comprehension of a topic to perform higher order thinking. In other words, to apply knowledge to new situations (syntheses), it is assumed that the student has knowledge with which to work.

Understand the interactions of people and the physical environment.
    1.1 Construct a habitat to attract birds to the school campus.

This is an example of an objective that addresses the same standard as did the earlier example, but at a higher level of thinking. To complete this objective, students would need to understand that human impact on the school site has taken away some of land animals previously used for habitats. They also will need to know what types of plants attract birds and what those plants require to grow successfully.

Remember, too, that an objective describes student responses that occur *after*, not during, instruction. Objectives state what students can do as a result of the knowledge and skills gained from the learning situation. Teachers help students learn new information and skills for reasons beyond knowledge acquisition. New facts are not ends, but rather means.

 # Reality Check

Question: Why write goals and objectives?

Creating a good lesson plan shows that some thought has gone into what is being taught; the goals and objectives are right there if anyone questions what the teacher is doing.

Dru Clarke
Teacher Consultant
Kansas

IN SUMMARY

New information is learned so that students can do something with the knowledge that they were not able to do before the learning experience. For example, students don't learn the alphabet so that they can recite or sing it. They learn the alphabet so that they can eventually apply that knowledge to learn to read. Similarly, students don't just learn that nature and humans interact. They learn about the impact of that interaction in order to take some actions: build wildlife sanctuaries, or predict dangerous weather patterns so they will know when to take shelter. Deciding what students will do with the newly acquired information is part of the lesson planning process and occurs at the point of writing goals and objectives.

UNIT CONNECTION

A unit plan will have more goals and objectives than does a single lesson because a unit contains more content and more lessons. Even though there are more objectives, they should still relate to the academic standards of the unit. It is important to keep the objectives broad enough to allow students to personalize them.

YOUR TURN

ACTIVITY 1: Distinguishing Between Goals and Objectives and Identifying Taxonomy Levels

INTASC Principles 2, 3, 6, and 7

Directions:

- Read the following statements.
- Identify the statements as lesson objectives or goal statements. <u>Underline</u> the active and measurable verb in the objectives. If you do not underline any verb, you are indicating that the statement is a goal.
- If the statement is a lesson objective, identify the associated cognitive level by writing the level on the line to the left of the statement.

Example:

_____ A. Use standard units of measurement

<u>application</u> B. *Measure* the length of the chalkboard to the nearest foot.

  A. A broad, general statement or goal. It does not use a verb that describes a specific, observable student response.

B. An objective. The verb *measure* describes a specific, observable student response. *Measure* is at the application level of the Taxonomy because it requires a student to apply (use) what he or she has learned in a specific situation.

Now it is your turn to distinguish between the goals and objectives, then identify taxonomy levels.

   _____   1. Understand the process of adding whole numbers together in columns.

   _____   2. Describe the symmetrical physical characteristics of a butterfly.

   _____   3. Comprehend the relationship between marine and land mammals.

   _____   4. Learn the process for solving word problems.

   _____   5. Illustrate the sequence of a story.

   _____   6. Demonstrate the steps of simple multiplication problems.

   _____   7. Realize the importance of providing areas for natural habitat.

   _____   8. Diagram the basic parts of a ship.

   _____   9. Evaluate the impact of water erosion on landforms over time.

   _____   10. Identify the elemental properties of water.

   _____   11. Map the major rivers of North America.

   _____   12. Develop an appreciation of reading.

 ACTIVITY 2: Writing an Instructional Objective

INTASC Principles 2, 3, 6, and 7

Directions:

1. Using the academic standard you selected in chapter 3, write a goal for your lesson.

   Example: Understand the interactions of people and the physical environment.

2. Using the academic standard you selected in chapter 3, decide what you want your students to be able to do after your instruction. Look at the Taxonomy in the application, analysis, synthesis, and evaluation levels. Write one or more specific student responses.

   Example:

   <u>Map</u> the school campus, identifying examples of man-made and naturally occurring items (buildings, hedges, trees, parking lots, playground).
   <u>Construct</u> a habitat to attract birds to the school campus.

3. Use the goal and specific student responses to form an instructional objective.

   Example:

   Understand the interactions of people and the physical environment.
       1.1 Map the school campus, identifying examples of man-made and naturally occurring items (buildings, hedges, trees, parking lots, playground).
       1.2 Construct a habitat to attract birds to the school campus.

ACTIVITY 3: Reflection

INTASC Principle 9

Directions: Write a brief response to the following questions.

1. What decisions did you have to make to write your lesson objective?

2. Did the process of writing an objective change your view of the teaching profession? Why or why not?

3. In what way do you have a more clear understanding of the direction your lesson will take?

REFERENCES

Bloom, B. S. (Ed.), Engelhart, M. D., Furst, E. J., Hill, W. H., & Krathwohl, D. R. (1956). *Taxonomy of educational objectives handbook 1: Cognitive domain.* New York: David McKay.

Florida Department of Education. (2005). *Florida's academic standards.* Retrieved June 13, 2005, from http://www.firn.edu/doe/menu/sss. htm.

Gronlund, N. (2004). *Writing instructional objectives for teaching and assessment* (7th ed.). Upper Saddle River, NJ: Merrill/Prentice Hall.

Indiana Department of Education. (2004). *Indiana's academic standards.* Retrieved June 13, 2005, from http://www.doe.state.in.us/.

Jacobsen, D., Eggen, P., & Kauchak, D (2002). *Methods for teaching: Promoting student learning* (6th ed.). Upper Saddle River, NJ: Merrill/ Prentice Hall.

Mager, R. (1962). *Preparing instructional objectives.* Belmont, CA: Fearon.

Marzano, R. J., Pickering, D. J., & Pollock, J. E. (2001). *Classroom instruction that works: Research-based strategies for increasing student achievement.* Alexandria, VA: ASCD.

National Council of Teachers of English & the International Reading Association. (1996). *Standards for the English language arts.* Urbana, IL: National Council of Teachers of English. Available at http://www.readwritethink.org/ standards.

National Council for the Social Studies. (1994). *Expectations of experience: Curriculum standards for social studies.* Washington, D.C.: National Council for the Social Studies. Available at http:// www.socialstudies.org/standards/.

National Council of Teachers of Mathematics. (1989). *Curriculum and evaluation standards for school mathematics.* Reston, VA: National Council of Teachers of Mathematics. Available at http://standards.nctm.org/.

National Research Council. (1996). *National science education standards.* Washington, D.C.: National Academy Press. Available at http:// www.nsta.org/.

Skinner, B. F. (1976). *About behaviorism.* New York: Vintage Books.

Tyler, R. (1949). *Basic principles of curriculum and instruction.* Chicago: University of Chicago Press.

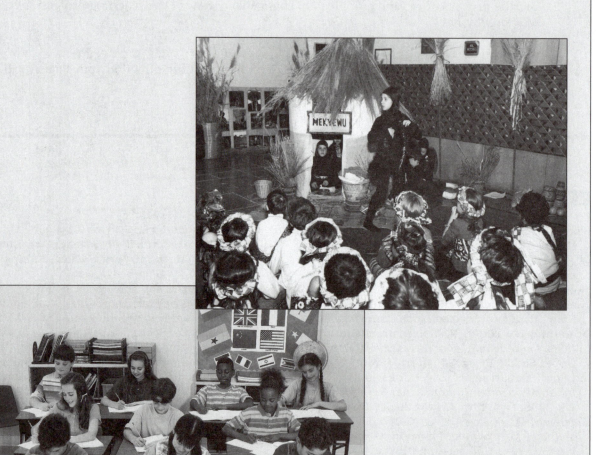

Designing Formative and Summative Assessments

Objective: Assess student learning.

1.1 Write one preassessment.
1.2 Write one formative assessment.
1.3 Write one summative assessment.

Using our road trip analogy, a scrapbook represents a lesson's summative assessment. A scrapbook documents the trip (Figure 5.1, p. 60). Summative assessments document student learning. Formative assessments compare to checks of the roadmap during the trip to verify the trip is "on track."

Relevant INTASC Principles: #1, #2, #3, #6, #7, #8 (See inside back cover.)

THE IMPORTANCE OF ASSESSMENT

Accountability has become a main focus of educational debate and policy development in recent years. This emphasis on accountability has led states to develop standards to describe the academic performance expected of K–12 students in each subject at each grade level. Many states have also developed standards for teachers— indicators of the knowledge, skills, and dispositions expected of teachers who are licensed to teach in that state. Many view teachers' ability to affect the performance of their students as representing the ultimate test of teacher preparation.

The National Council for Accreditation of Teacher Education (NCATE) is a national accrediting body for schools, colleges, and departments of education authorized by the U.S. Department of Education. NCATE determines which schools, colleges, and

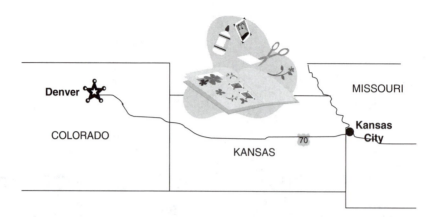

FIGURE 5.1 Documenting the Road Trip Experiences

departments of education meet rigorous national standards in preparing teachers and other school specialists for the classroom. Embedded throughout the NCATE 2000 standards is the expectation that teacher candidates are able to demonstrate that they actually have an impact on student learning. For example, in NCATE Standard 1, which deals with candidate knowledge, skills, and dispositions, the following behavior is expected for teacher candidates:

> Teacher candidates accurately assess and analyze student learning, make appropriate adjustments to instruction, monitor student learning, and have a positive effect on learning for all students. . . . Candidates for all professional education roles are expected to demonstrate positive effects on student learning. Teachers and teacher candidates have student learning as the focus of their work. Throughout the program, teacher candidates develop knowledge bases for analyzing student learning and practice by collecting data and assessing student learning through case studies, field experiences, and other experiences. They might examine student work samples for evidence of learning and develop lesson plans to help students who are having problems understanding concepts being taught. Student learning should be demonstrated directly by all teacher candidates during clinical practice. (NCATE, 2000, p. 16)

This statement very clearly describes the expectation that those who are preparing to become teachers must be able to demonstrate they can positively affect the learning and performance of those they teach.

Implicit in the call for demonstrating impact on student learning is the need for accurately measuring student learning and for determining how learning and performance are related to specific teaching behaviors. Clearly, it is important to equip teacher candidates with the necessary tools to assess and analyze student learning.

REASONS FOR CLASSROOM ASSESSMENT

Assessment can serve many purposes. Cruickshank, Bainer, and Metcalf (1999) identify two main reasons: (1) to provide information about the effectiveness of a teacher's instruction, and (2) to provide information about students' performance. So assessment can answer two very important questions for teachers, which are intertwined: How did I do? And how did my students do?

It is important for teachers to know how well selected teaching strategies worked in helping students accomplish a lesson's goals and objectives. In chapter 1, we discussed the importance of teachers being reflective practitioners. One of the things on which to reflect is the effectiveness of instruction. One way for any teacher to examine his effectiveness is to examine his students' performance on his own teacher-created assessments and to ask himself the following questions: Did most students reach mastery? What about those students who did not? How will I remediate instruction for those who didn't reach mastery? Is there a more effective method for teaching the content next time?

Performance on assessments is important information for the students themselves as well. To improve their learning, they need to receive feedback from their teachers. "The most powerful single modification that enhances achievement is feedback" (Hattie, 1992, p. 9).

As a result of reviewing numerous research studies that looked into the effectiveness of providing feedback to students, Marzano, Pickering, and Pollock (2001) recommend that feedback should be corrective, criterion-referenced, and timely. Corrective feedback provides students with information about what they did correctly as well as about what they did incorrectly. Criterion-referenced feedback tells students how they did relative to specific skills or knowledge as identified in the teacher's lesson plan objectives and goals. It does not tell the students how they did compared to others in the class.

Feedback should also be provided in a timely manner. In general, the greater the delay in providing feedback, the less effective it will be for students. Jarolimek, Foster, and Kellough (2005) caution that it is important to tell students that the "object of assessment in schools is learner *performance* and not to evaluate individuals as human beings" (p. 250). This is an important reminder for all teachers.

One other reason to assess student learning is to demonstrate a teacher's impact on her students' learning. The importance of this reason is made clear at the beginning of this chapter. But how can a teacher demonstrate impact on student learning? One way is to create, use, and compare the results of parallel pre- and postassessments.

Assessments should be developed before finishing the lesson planning process. Why? Because if you don't know where the lesson is going, how the students will demonstrate their learning, then how can you begin a lesson? Creating assessments during the planning process, instead of waiting until instruction has begun or even ended, helps bring focus to the lesson. In addition, the teacher can clearly explain expectations to students at the beginning of a lesson so they know what is expected of them. So, once the topic is selected, the standards identified, the goals and objectives written, informational and instructional sources studied, assessments must be created. Begin with the end in mind. But before you can create your assessments, you'll need to understand some terminology. We'll return to the process later in this chapter.

ASSESSMENT AND EVALUATION

The terms *assessment* and *evaluation* are often used interchangeably. In fact, Roberts and Kellough (2004) consider the terms to be synonymous. According to Martin-Kniep (2000), **assessment** refers to all teacher efforts to document students' learning before, during, and after instruction. **Evaluation** refers to the process of interpretation, reflection, and decision making based on assessment results (Marchant, Powell, & Schoenfeldt, 2003). In this book, assessment refers to documenting student learning. Evaluation refers to the analysis of that documentation in order to make decisions about student learning and teacher instruction. Regardless of whether one believes the terms assessment and evaluation represent separate actions or that the terms are synonymous, they are, at the very least, part of the same process.

Types of Assessment

Certain key terms are helpful to create assessments and to understand the language used by educators. **Traditional assessments** refer to most paper-and-pencil tests or exams. These can include multiple choice, matching, and true-false items, what most people think of first when thinking of classroom assessment. It is important to know, though, that there are many other ways to assess student learning. These "other ways" are often referred to as

 Reality Check

Question: What do you think about assessments?

Assessment is an essential part of the educational process. . . . Knowing how to gauge my assessment derives from my need to develop and enhance lessons that are student-centered and standards-based, meeting the needs of all learner types in my classroom.

Bryan Fountain
Loogootee Elementary
Third grade

alternative assessments because they represent an alternative to traditional assessments. Alternative assessments are sometimes called *authentic, active, aligned,* or *direct assessments* (Jarolimek et al., 2005). **Performance assessments** require students to perform a task that demonstrates their understanding by applying their knowledge to a particular situation (McBrien & Brandt, 1997). These types of assessment have more than one right answer or solution. Examples of performance assessments include photo essays, a detailed illustration, a political cartoon, a poem or song lyrics, a map, a story, a model, or a PowerPoint presentation.

After studying how to calculate an area, a teacher might ask the students to measure the amount of carpet needed for the classroom, examine the types of carpet available, figure out the cost of several types, and then make a recommendation of which carpet is the best buy. This process uses higher order thinking skills than if students were simply asked to use the algorithm for figuring area to solve a set of problems from a textbook. Performance tasks such as the carpet example can also be used during instruction. Performance assessment and performance tasks, which can also be used for assessment, attempt to make learning more authentic to help students not only learn how to do something, but to apply that learning in real-life, problem-solving situations.

It is also possible to *differentiate assessment products* to meet the individual needs of the learners. This can be done by considering

Reality Check

Question: How do you assess learning?

There are so many ways to assess children in addition to paper-and-pencil tests, and I believe several means of assessment *should be used* in order to really understand the strengths and weaknesses of children. Daily observations, daily work, and special projects can assess children and determine growth and understanding. Portfolios (digital and paper) can show progress over time. Asking children to explain their thinking or asking them to show how they got the answer can often shed much light on what children know, as well as asking children if they agree or disagree with a given answer, idea, etc., and explaining why they agree or disagree. This can help teachers know how to change instruction to fit needs!

"Show me" kinds of tests are often more appropriate than paper and pencil, especially if children are nonreaders or low readers. For example, if we want to assess a child's math skills, we need to be sure we are doing that and *not* testing reading ability. Asking children to explain their answer to a math problem can show the teacher what the child does/does not understand. Many times children know the answer to a math problem if someone reads it to them, but they might get the answer wrong if they cannot read the problem independently. Using a variety of assessments can add validity and support for teacher judgments, in addition to using paper-and-pencil tests.

Jolena Sutherland
Grades 2–3 Looping
Burris Laboratory School

student readiness, interest, or learning profiles. In differentiating lesson products by readiness, teachers generally create three levels or tiers of difficulty that correspond to learners that work below, at, or above grade level. Though the students are all creating a product that demonstrates their understanding of the lesson's content, those working below grade level will work at a more concrete level than the other two groups. In differentiating the lesson's product by student interest, a teacher provides several options from which children choose the one way that most interests them. Teachers can also offer product options based on learner profile, for example, offering options that appeal to various intelligences identified by Howard Gardner (1993). For additional information on Gardner's Multiple Intelligences, see Figure 6.3 in chapter 6.

THE ASSESSMENT PROCESS: PREASSESSMENT, FORMATIVE, AND SUMMATIVE ASSESSMENT

Assessment is an ongoing process that occurs before, during, and after instruction. **Preassessments** are used before teaching to determine the level of understanding of each student. Information gathered is used by teachers during the lesson planning process. If, for example, a teacher had selected the stages of development of a butterfly as a lesson topic and found in the preassessment that the children already knew the stages, she could change the emphasis of the lesson. Perhaps she could begin her lesson with a review of the life stages of a butterfly and move more quickly into a comparison of the life stages of humans with those of butterflies. Preassessments, then, are used for diagnostic purposes to determine students' knowledge and skills before beginning new instruction.

There are many ways to preassess student learning. One commonly used method is called a K-W-L chart. The K stands for what is already *known*; the W for what a child *wants to learn*; and the L for what a child *learned*. Reading what each child placed in his K and W columns will help a teacher determine what that child already knows about an upcoming topic as well as what the child would like to learn. Both pieces of information are useful in creating lesson plans. Sometimes teachers use one K-W-L chart to record class answers, but that doesn't identify what each *individual* child knows. If possible, it is better to have each child complete the K and W for himself. The L can be filled in at the end of a lesson.

For children who can't write, there are still ways to preassess student learning. *Drawings* provide one method (substitute terms for "drawings" include *illustration, sketch, diagram,* etc.). If a teacher is preparing a lesson about an insect's body parts, he could ask each student to draw an insect, showing all the parts. While examining each drawing, the teacher could individually ask each child to tell him the names of the body parts. The teacher could record the child's responses on the drawing or on the back. Drawings can, of course, also be used with students who can write.

Observation is another way to preassess learning. If a teacher is planning a lesson on patterning, she could set out two sizes of manipulatives, arrange a series of the shapes in an A-B pattern, and then ask children to reproduce and name the pattern and choose the next shape needed to extend the pattern. Children who understand the pattern might say, "The pattern goes big/little; big/little; and the next one will be a big shape." A checklist can be used to record student responses. Beside each child's name, the teacher could mark a "+" to indicate the child could identify and repeat the pattern and a "−" to indicate that a child could not.

Formative assessment occurs during instruction. Formative assessment provides students with feedback as they experiment with new content and skills. Teachers should also encourage students to self-assess in order to personalize the learning and decide what they need to spend more time examining or practicing. Research shows that high-quality formative assessment has a powerful, positive impact on student learning (Black & William, 1998). Unfortunately, research also shows that few teachers use high-quality formative assessment. Grades are overemphasized, whereas giving useful feedback is underemphasized (Black & William, 1998). Formative assessment can be accomplished through observation of students and by asking questions structured to check for specific understanding of concepts. Formative assessments are not generally graded or scored, but are used to gather information on student progress to provide corrective feedback.

Questions should be developed during the lesson planning process. Don't try to create them while you teach. Teachers who do not prepare questions during planning tend to ask more low-level cognitive questions (Wilen, 1991), or questions that are vague or that are not developmentally appropriate. The levels of Bloom's Taxonomy for the cognitive domain can guide you in creating a range of questions. Good questioning recognizes the wide possibilities of thought and incorporates several levels (Sanders, 1966).

Summative assessment occurs at the end of the learning process. In addition, high-stakes tests such as state assessments, the ACT, and the SAT are examples of summative assessments. Lesson and unit posttests are summative assessments. Summative assessments in classrooms are usually scored, recorded, and reported. In elementary classrooms, summative assessment results are used to create report cards and discussed at parent-teacher conferences.

Evaluation

In traditional paper-and-pencil tests, evaluation of student learning is done through scoring or grading of the student work. The score is usually reported as a percentage correct of total possible

Reality Check

Question: What is the importance of assessment?

A critical piece of assessment is student involvement. Students take more ownership of their learning when I give them targeted, specific feedback. Students seem more motivated to set goals when they have opportunities to reflect on their own work.

Terri Durgan
Quail Run Elementary
Fourth grade

responses. Many teachers view this as being the most objective way to evaluate student learning. It is either correct or incorrect. One criticism of this type of assessment is that classroom testing of this type encourages rote and superficial learning (Black & William, 1998).

Performance assessments are usually graded with a rubric. A **rubric** is a scoring instrument that evaluates a student's performance on a range of criteria rather than providing a single numerical score. A rubric is created to try to make subjective judgments about the quality of a student product more objective.

A copy of the scoring rubric is handed out to students before the lesson begins to get students to think about the criteria on which their final work will be judged. If you walked into a university class and were told by the instructor that a quiz would be given at the end of class and that you'd be able to use any notes that you took during class, perhaps you would take different notes than if you were not so informed. The same type of thinking lies behind providing rubrics to students before a lesson begins. When students receive rubrics beforehand, they understand how they will be evaluated and can prepare accordingly.

CREATING A RUBRIC

There are two main types of rubric: holistic and analytic (Marchant et al., 2003). **Analytic rubrics** identify and assess individual components of a finished product. (See the example in Figure 5.2.) **Holistic rubrics** assign a level of performance by assessing a combined set of criteria. (See the example in Figure 5.3.) Analytic rubrics are generally more common because teachers want to assess each criterion separately, particularly for assignments that involve a larger number of criteria. It becomes more and more difficult to assign a level of performance in a holistic rubric as the number of criteria increases. Look at the sample holistic rubric in Figure 5.3.

	Beginning	**Developing**	**Accomplished**
Characters	Not all main characters used in the retelling	All main characters used in the retelling	All main characters and important minor characters used in the retelling
Sequence of Events	Retells story out of sequence	Retells story in correct sequence leaving out some important parts of the story	Retells story in correct sequence leaving out no important parts of story
Voice Quality	Speaks too softly, too quickly, or mumbles	Usually speaks loudly, slowly, and clearly	Speaks loudly, slowly, and clearly throughout the retelling

FIGURE 5.2 Sample Analytic Rubric

At what level would you place a child who spoke clearly, loudly, and slowly throughout the retelling, used all the main characters but no minor characters in the retelling, and yet told the story out of sequence?

Accomplished

- Retells story in correct sequence and includes all important parts of the story.
- Speaks loudly, slowly, and clearly throughout the retelling.
- Uses all main characters and important minor characters in the retelling.

Developing

- Retells story in correct sequence, but leaves out some important parts of the story.
- Usually speaks loudly, slowly, and clearly.
- Uses all main characters in the retelling.

Beginning

- Retells story out of sequence.
- Speaks too softly, too quickly, or mumbles.
- Omits some main characters in the retelling.

FIGURE 5.3 Sample Holistic Rubric

TECHNOLOGY IN EDUCATION

View sample rubrics and create your own online:

The 6 +1 Trait Writing Method (Northwest Regional Education Library, 2006), commonly used in elementary classrooms, utilizes analytic rubrics to assess students' written work. For more information go to http://www.nwrel.org/assessment/pdfRubrics/6plus1traits.pdf.

Also:

Rubristar: http://rubistar.4teachers.org/index.php.

Teachnology: http://www.teach-nology.com/web_tools/rubrics/.

Rubric Builder: http://landmark-project.com/classweb/tools/rubric_builder.php. http://landmark-project.com/rubric_builder/index. php.

In developing either type of rubric, it is necessary to identify the components of the task and the levels of performance, and provide clear indicators for each level of performance. In primary grades, rubrics often define levels of performance using words such as *beginning, developing,* and *accomplished.* Other terms used might be *unsatisfactory, basic, proficient,* and *distinguished.* Points can also be assigned to each level. Often-used configurations of numbering systems are a 1–3 or 1–4 scale. Figure 5.2 shows part of an analytic rubric that could be used to score oral retelling of a story. Figure 5.3 depicts a sample holistic rubric that could be used to score oral retelling of a story.

A PROCESS FOR MEASURING TEACHER IMPACT

Embedded throughout the NCATE 2000 standards is the expectation that teacher candidates are able to demonstrate that they actually have an impact on student learning. How can a teacher demonstrate that impact? As mentioned earlier in this chapter, one way is to create, use, and compare the results of parallel pre- and postassessments (Marchant et al., 2003). Parallel tests agree in number and types of items as well as in range of difficulty of questions asked. If you create an easier pretest than posttest, students will likely perform more poorly on the posttest. The test results might look as if the students didn't learn much or even "lost ground" from pre- to posttest. The questions should be similar and relate to the lesson's standards, but not identical. Ideally, pre- and posttests should be interchangeable. See Figure 5.4 for sample parallel items.

Academic Standard: Properties of Matter

Test 1

1. At what temperature, measured in degrees Fahrenheit, does water freeze?
2. Name a solid other than ice.
3. When a liquid changes to a gas, the process is called
   _____ .
4. Molecules are closest together in which state of matter?
   a. Gas
   b. Liquid
   c. Solid

Test 2

1. At what temperature, measured in degrees Fahrenheit, does water boil?
2. Name a liquid other than water.
3. When a gas changes to a liquid, the process is called
   _____ .
4. Molecules are most free to move around in which state of matter?
   a. Gas
   b. Liquid
   c. Solid

FIGURE 5.4 Sample Parallel Assessment Items

Determine a "passing" percentage. Administer the pretest. Record the scores for each student. Use Excel or another similar program to graph the results. Create a bar graph that shows each child's average pretest performance. Also include a bar that shows the class average. Identify the passing percentage on the graph with a line. Analyze the results before completing your lesson plan. Did some students surpass the "pass" score? Will you need to include more background information? Will you need to work with certain students to help them with some prerequisite knowledge that other students already know?

Create your lesson plan, incorporating the information you gained from the pretest results. Teach the lesson. Administer the posttest. Graph the results as you did for the pretest. Compare the pre- and posttest results for each student individually as well as the class average. Did the students show improvement from pre to post? Did any student results stand out? How? Will you need to reteach some students? A graph brings focus to assessment results. It is easier to see at a glance the achievement of each student. Then you can go back to the actual tests to see what items were answered incorrectly.

IN SUMMARY

Traditionally teachers give posttests to determine student performance. But without pretest results, it is impossible to say if student performance is due to the lesson. Some students may have already known the content. The pre–posttest comparison does not need to be done for each lesson, but should be done as often as time allows. But some type of preassessment is absolutely necessary during the lesson planning process before the plan is finalized if a teacher hopes to meet the needs of all students and discover her or his instructional impact on student learning.

 ## UNIT CONNECTION

A unit provides an excellent opportunity to measure your impact on your students' learning. When developing pre- and postassessments, it will be necessary to include multiple test items for each standard. Otherwise, the results will not be very meaningful. If, for example, you only ask one question for the content of one standard, a student can only receive 100% or 0%. If two questions are used for each standard, then the possible scores are 100%, 50%, or 0%. It seems logical that in designing the pre- and postassessments, at least 4 questions should be used to assess the content of each standard.

The graphs created to examine student knowledge will need to be arranged a bit differently than those for a single lesson. The results for all items that assess each standard should be combined. Then a graph would show each student's performance on each of the unit's selected standards. The class averages likewise would need to reflect the group's average performance of each standard.

 # YOUR TURN

✏ ACTIVITY 1: Create Your Lesson's Pre- and Postassessments

INTASC Principles 1, 2, 3, and 8

Directions: Complete the following elements of your lesson plan:

1. Lesson topic
2. Lesson's academic standard(s)
3. Lesson objective(s)
4. Method of assessing learning
5. Identify the criteria that indicate a "passing" score.
6. Create the preassessment.
7. Create the postassessment.

Sample Completed Activity 1

1. **Topic:** Insects

2. **Academic Standard:** Demonstrate that living things can be sorted into groups using various features.

3. **Objective:** Understand that living things can be sorted into groups.

    1.1 Identify the body parts of insects.

4. **Method:** Identify the parts of an insect on a drawing.

5. **Criteria:** 100% correct; the drawing must show an insect's three main body parts, two antennae, and six legs.

6. **Preassessment instructions** (to be read aloud): We are going to be studying insects next week. Today, I'd like to see what you already know about insects. First, print your name on the piece of paper you have been given. (pause) Now draw an insect on the paper. You can draw any insect you'd like as long as it is an insect. Make it look as real as you can. Be sure to draw all the body parts of your insect. When you are finished with your drawing, raise your hand. I will come get your drawing and ask you to tell me the names of the body parts and the type of insect you have drawn. You may use crayons or a pencil or both to complete your drawing. (*Note:* File the preassessment drawings in a folder until after the children complete the postassessment drawings.)

7. **Postassessment instructions** (to be read aloud): We have been studying insects this week. Today, I'd like to see what you have learned about insects. First, print your name on the piece of paper you have been given. (pause) Now draw an insect on the paper. You can draw any insect you'd like as long as it is an insect. Make it look as real as you can. Be sure to draw all the body parts of your insect. You may use crayons or a pencil or both to complete your drawing. Then, using the word box on the top of the page, find the word for each body part and write it next to the correct part of the insect.

 ACTIVITY 2: Create a Rubric

INTASC Principles 1, 2, 3, and 8

Directions:

1. Create an analytic rubric that could be used to assess your pre- and postassessments. Because the pre- and postassessments are parallel and measure the same learning outcomes, you will create and use only one rubric. You can generate your own rubric or use one of the Web sites identified in the TiE box in this chapter.

Sample Analytic Rubric for Activity 2

	Beginning	**Developing**	**Accomplished**
Body Parts	One body part is drawn	Two body parts are drawn	Three body parts are drawn
Legs and Antennae	Two legs drawn	3–5 legs drawn	Six legs/two antennae
Identification	Can name one body part	Can name the two body parts drawn	Can name the three body parts drawn

ACTIVITY 3: Create a Formative Assessment

INTASC Principles 1, 2, 3, and 8

Directions: Complete the following:

1. Create a list of questions that you could use during the learning process that would help you determine students' level of understanding. The questions should represent at least three of the cognitive levels identified in Bloom's Taxonomy.

2. Identify the level in parentheses after the question. At least one question should have more than one possible correct answer.

3. Include expected responses to each question you pose.

Sample Formative Assessment for Activity 3

Sample questions to be used during instruction:

1. Name the three body parts of an insect. (knowledge level)

   Answer: Head, abdomen, thorax

2. Why is a spider not an insect? (comprehension)

   Answer: Spiders have eight legs and insects have six legs.

3. In your opinion, which insect is the most useful? Why? (evaluation)

   Answer: Answers will vary, but will contain the name of an insect and at least one reason it is useful. For example, a student may reply that bees are useful because they make honey that people use.

 ACTIVITY 4A: Differentiating Your Lesson's Product by Readiness

INTASC Principles 1, 2, 3, and 8

Directions: Complete the following:

1. Identify your lesson's grade level, subject, and objective.

2. Create three tiers for your lesson's product:

   Tier 1: beginning learners
   Tier 2: at-grade-level learners
   Tier 3: advanced learners

   Your lesson's preassessment results will help you know which students will be working at which "tier" for this content. All students are using the same types of materials and creating similar products. Only their level of readiness is tiered.

Sample Activity 4A

Grade Level:　5

Subject:　Math

Objective:　Compare fractional parts.

　1.1 Sort proper and improper fractions.

Materials:　Each pair or small group of students will be given a set of 10 index cards. An improper or proper fraction is written on each. Tiers 2 and 3 will also have cards that equal 1, such as 4/4 and 9/9.

Tier 1:　Students will create a T-Chart, labeling one side "Proper Fractions" and the other "Improper Fractions." Students will then place the index cards under the correct labels.

Tier 2:　Students will create a table with three columns, labeling one as "proper fractions," one as "improper fractions," and one as "equals 1." Students will place their index cards in the proper sections.

Tier 3:　Students will create a number line and place their index cards in numerical order and in the correct location on the number line.

 ACTIVITY 4B: Differentiating Your Lesson's Product by Interest

INTASC Principles 1, 2, 3, and 8

Directions: Create three options for your lesson's product. At the end of instruction, allow the students to select which product they would like to produce. Student interest is the basis for product selection.

Option 1—

Option 2—

Option 3—

Sample Activity 2

Grade Level:　High School

Subject:　English

Objective:　Become a better writer.

　1.1. Select an organizational structure for a piece of writing.

Material/s:　*Night* by Elie Wiesel (1982)

Option 1:　Create daily diary entries for an entire week that represents Moshe the Beadle's time in the forest of Galicia.

Option 2:　Create a poem that Elie Wiesel might have written that explains his thoughts about Moshe and Moshe's descriptions of what transpired in the forest of Galicia.

Option 3:　Create a Polish newspaper article that describes the incidents in the forest.

ACTIVITY 4C: Differentiating Your Lesson's Product by Learner Profile

INTASC Principles 1, 2, 3, and 8

Directions:

A lesson's product is the method used by students to demonstrate their understanding of the new content and is a form of assessment. For this activity:

1. Create a list of possible products for your lesson that would utilize at least three of Gardner's Multiple Intelligences.

   Option 1—

   Option 2—

   Option 3—

Look at the following list of sample lesson products for ideas. Make them more specific to reflect the content of your lesson. You can create your own options as well. Students with interpersonal intelligence preferences can be offered the opportunity to work in a pair or group situation, choosing one of the options listed in one of the other categories. Students with intrapersonal preferences can work alone, choosing one of the options that represent one of the other intelligences. Find more information on Multiple Intelligences by looking ahead in this book to chapter 6.

Possible Lesson Products

Verbal/Linguistic	**Visual/Spatial**
Poem or story	Model
Editorial	Chart
Oral report/speech	Mural
Logical/Mathematical	**Bodily/Kinesthetic**
Advertisement	Pantomime
Database	Play
Graph or diagram	Collage
Naturalist	**Interpersonal**
Scientific drawing	Work with others
Artifact collection	Create a game
Diorama	
Intrapersonal	**Musical**
Work alone	Choral reading
Persuasive speech	Song
	Dance

Sample Activity 4C

Grade Level: 2

Subject: Science

Objective: Understand that dinosaurs had distinguishing physical characteristics.

1.1. Sort dinosaurs by some distinguishing characteristic(s).

Option 1 (Musical):   Create new lyrics to a known tune to identify various dinosaurs.

Option 2 (Bodily/Kinesthetic):   Act out, using sound effects, various types of dinosaurs.

Option 3 (Verbal/Linguistic):   Write a story about different types of dinosaurs meeting at a watering hole.

Option 4 (Logical/Mathematical):   Create a chart to compare various dinosaurs using one or more distinguishing characteristics.

 ACTIVITY 5: Reflection

INTASC Principle 9

Directions: Write a brief response to the following questions.

1. What decisions did you have to make when writing your lesson's assessments?

2. Did the process change your view of the teaching profession? Why or why not?

3. Explain whether you now have a clearer understanding of the direction your lesson will take.

REFERENCES

Black, P., & William, D. (1998). Inside the black box: Raising standards through classroom assessment. *Phi Delta Kappan, 80*(2), 139–148.

Cruickshank, D., Bainer, D., & Metcalf, K. (1999). *The act of teaching* (2nd ed.). Boston: McGraw-Hill College.

Gardner, H. (1993). *Multiple intelligences: The theory in practice.* New York: Basic Books.

Hattie, J. (1992). Measuring the effects of schooling. *Australian Journal of Education, 36*(1), 5–13.

Jarolimek, J., Foster, C., & Kellough, R. (2005). *Teaching and learning in the elementary school* (8th ed.) Upper Saddle River, NJ: Merrill/Prentice Hall.

Marchant, G., Powell, J., & Schoenfeldt, M. (2003). *The learning assessment model manual: A rubrics-based work sample assessment tool.* Retrieved April 25, 2006, from http://www.bsu.edu/tcapps/uas/lamp/default.asp?

Martin-Kniep, G. (2000). *Becoming a better teacher: Eight innovations that work.* Alexandria, VA: Association for Supervision and Curriculum Development.

Marzano, R. J., Pickering, D. J., & Pollock, J. E. (2001). *Classroom instruction that works: Research-based strategies for increasing student achievement.* Alexandria, VA: Association for Supervision and Curriculum Development.

McBrien, J., & Brandt, R. (1997). *The language of learning: A guide to education terms.* Alexandria, VA: Association for Supervision and Curriculum Development.

National Council for the Accreditation of Teacher Education. (2000). *NCATE 2000 unit standards.* Washington, D.C.: Author.

Northwest Regional Educational Library. *6 + 1 trait writing assessment.* Retrieved April 21, 2006, from http://www.nwrel.org/assessment/pdf Rubrics/6plus1traits.PDF.

Roberts, P. L., & Kellough, R. D. (2004). *A guide for developing interdisciplinary thematic units* (3rd ed). Upper Saddle River, NJ: Merrill/Prentice Hall.

Sanders, N. (1966). *Classroom questions: What kinds?* New York: Harper & Row.

Wilen, W. (1991). *Questioning skills for teachers: What research says to the teacher* (3rd ed.). Washington, D.C.: National Education Association. (ED 332 983).

Choosing the Lesson Content and Instructional Strategies

Objective: Become knowledgeable about the lesson's content.

1.1 Find and list informational sources.

1.2 Find and list instructional sources.

Using our road trip analogy, choosing the lesson content corresponds to creating a file that contains travel books, brochures, and Internet sites that help the travelers decide how to "get the most out of" the trip (Figure 6.1, p. 78).

Relevant INTASC Principles: #1, #2, #3, #4, #5, #6, #7, #8, #9, #10 (See inside back cover of this book for complete list.)

A HIGHLY QUALIFIED TEACHER IN EVERY CLASSROOM

Who dares to teach must never cease to learn.

—John Cotton Dana

The No Child Left Behind Act (NCLB), viewed as the most sweeping federal education bill in more than 40 years, was signed into law in 2002. No Child Left Behind is the name for the reauthorized and amended Elementary and Secondary Education Act (ESEA) of 1965. A major objective of NCLB is to ensure that all students in American schools have highly qualified teachers. Well-prepared teachers have a great impact on student achievement. In fact, research demonstrates the clear correlation between student academic achievement and teacher quality (Sanders & Rivers, 1996). The NCLB law, therefore,

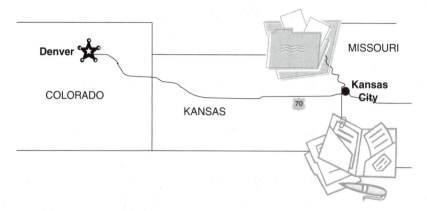

FIGURE 6.1   Researching Activity Ideas for the Road Trip

requires that teachers of core academic subjects meet three basic requirements:

- Hold a bachelor's degree.
- Obtain full state certification, which can be alternative certification.
- Demonstrate subject-matter competency in the core academic subjects taught.

The law identifies the core academic subjects as English, reading or language arts, mathematics, science, foreign languages, civics and government, economics, arts, history, and geography (U.S. Department of Education, 2007).

UNDERSTANDING CONTEXT: THE LEARNERS

When a teacher tries to teach something to the entire class, chances are $1/3$ already know it; $1/3$ will get it; and the remaining third won't. So $2/3$ of the students are wasting their time.

—Lillian Katz

 **TECHNOLOGY IN EDUCATION**

Go to the **No Child Left Behind** Web site. Read the law to see how it affects your career as a teacher: http://www.ed.gov/nclb/landing.jhtml.

Test yourself to see if you meet the requirements for a **highly qualified teacher.** Take a quiz at the Web site of the National Education Association: http://www.nea.org/esea/qualification/teacher/index.html.

We all learned in science class that no two snowflakes are alike. We also learned that no two sets of fingerprints are identical. Students in an elementary classroom are like snowflakes and fingerprints; they are not all alike. Some students struggle with learning while others find learning easy and often perform beyond the expectations for their assigned grade level. The rest of the students in a given classroom fall somewhere in between these two extremes. Academic diversity is evident in every classroom.

What can a teacher do to help each child in the classroom be successful? It is much easier to "teach to the middle," ignoring both the struggling students and those at the "top of the heap." Teachers often reason that the top students will challenge themselves and are able to learn on their own. However, recent research by the Davidson Institute (2003) has shown that one in every five high school dropouts typically tests in the gifted range. That means approximately 20% of dropouts are considered gifted, while it is generally recognized that approximately 5% of the student population nationwide are considered gifted (National Association of Gifted Children, 2006). So why would these "bright" students drop out? According to Tracy Cross, professor of gifted studies at Ball State University, "Problems typically arise when gifted children feel their work and talents are not valued by classmates (and) teachers" (Malone, 2004).

Teachers also often struggle with how to best help learners with special needs. If a student has a recognized disability, the child will have an Individualized Educational Program (IEP), which will outline the services that child will receive. The classroom teacher will work closely with the special education teacher to make necessary modifications and adaptations. It is imperative that we teach all the children in our classroom. Understanding how to differentiate instruction is one key to helping each child succeed.

WHAT IS DIFFERENTIATION?

"Differentiation is proactive; rooted in assessment; provides multiple approaches to content, process, and product; is student centered; and is a blend of whole-class, group, and individual instruction"

TECHNOLOGY IN EDUCATION

To get ideas for making lesson adaptations and modifications for **special needs learners** and to read about the various **areas of exceptionality,** go to the Council for Exceptional Children's Web site at http://www.cec.sped.org/.

(Tomlinson, 2001, pp. 3–5). Let's examine how those elements affect the lesson planning process. During the planning stage, proactive teachers think through what each student needs and how best to meet those needs. The teacher does this by preassessing each child.

Knowing what each child already knows about an upcoming topic or skill allows the teacher to plan more effectively. If, for example, the teacher is beginning to plan for teaching about facts and opinions and discovers in the pretest that 90% of the students passed at or above the predetermined "mastery level criteria," then she will design her instruction differently than if 90% of the students did not meet the mastery level. In the first scenario, the teacher will need to design special small group or individual lessons to help the 10% who didn't pass the pretest. In the second scenario, the teacher will need to plan for the 10% who are ready to move beyond basic information about facts and opinions. A teacher who is differentiating instruction plans a variety of approaches in the lesson's content, process, and product and is guided by knowledge of each individual student's strengths, weaknesses, interests, and learning style. Let's examine each of those terms separately.

UNDERSTANDING DIFFERENTIATION: IMPORTANT TERMS DEFINED

We all have ability. The difference is how we use it.
—Stevie Wonder

Teachers who use differentiation to meet the needs of all learners in their classrooms differentiate the *content, process,* and *product* of lessons. They do so by considering the *readiness, interests,* and *learning profile* of the students. They "tier" their lesson's content, process, or product. There are usually three tiers when differentiating by readiness. Tier one is for students with little prior knowledge or experience with the topic; tier two is for students working at grade level; and tier three is designed for students who are working above the expected level of readiness for the content. Principles of differentiation are being implemented to facilitate access to the curriculum by students of diverse abilities and needs (King-Sears, 2001). When teachers differentiate by interest or learner profile, options are selected by students. Refer to Figure 6.2 and read the definitions of the terms that follow.

Content

In this chapter, **content** will be defined as the "input" of a lesson. In other words, the content is what the teacher is trying to teach, and what the student is trying to learn. This content can be concepts,

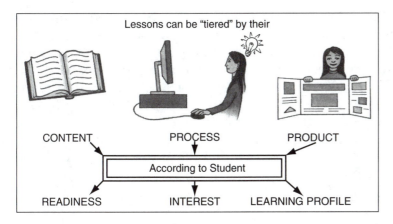

FIGURE 6.2 Tiered Lessons

principles, facts, or skills. A teacher who differentiates instruction can do so according to the lesson's content. "In an appropriately differentiated classroom all learners focus much of their time and attention on the key concepts, principles, and skills identified by the teacher as essential to growth and development in the subject—but at varying degrees of abstractness, complexity, open-endedness, problem clarity, and structure" (Kiernan [& Tomlinson], 1997).

For example, among a group of middle school students learning about elections, some students may be able to memorize and understand terms such as *candidates, primary, voting, registration, polling place, democracy, republic,* and *Electoral College,* and understand the connection of these terms to elections in the United States. Other students may learn not only those basic terms, but might compare elections in other democracies with those in the United States. They are ready to move beyond just the basics, but all the students will learn or perhaps review the basics. The fundamental content to be learned was found in the state and perhaps national content area standards and the district or school curriculum guidelines.

How did the teacher know who needed what? Though sometimes it seems easy to tell who knows what in a classroom, identifying what individual students know about each topic may surprise even a very experienced teacher. Instead, a teacher should determine what each child already knows through use of a pretest. A pretest can be a formal paper-and-pencil one, or the teacher can determine what each child knows by asking children to orally answer a few questions, through discussion, or observation. Once she knows the results, she can determine the readiness level of each child for that particular content. She may want to record anecdotal records or a checklist of the oral pretest replies to document individual student knowledge.

Process

In this chapter, **process** will be defined as the activities that students use to make sense of the content they are trying to learn. They use various processes to interact with or use the content while learning.

Most of the time the teacher offers a variety of sense-making activities; sometimes students may suggest an activity or method they would like to use. A teacher might suggest that students use a variety of written materials such as the social studies textbook, an encyclopedia, and a historical fiction book to gather information about elections. Or he might suggest an Internet site that offers a graphic overview of American elections. Students might also use flashcards to learn important terms. Viewing a DVD might be yet another type of information source for students to use to process the information to be learned.

Product

If content is the input, then the product is the output. A **product** shows how students have learned the concepts, principles, facts, or skills. A teacher who differentiates may offer students a variety of possible products from which to choose. A few ways that students might demonstrate their understanding of elections might include, for example, creating a poster, writing an essay, role playing, or creating a PowerPoint presentation.

Student Readiness

The term **readiness** is defined here as the ability level of each student with respect to learning the task at hand. Readiness is affected by a child's learning rate and prior experiences. All toddlers don't take their first steps at the exact same age or utter their first words at the same age, nor are their first words the same. Teachers realize that students in a classroom do not all learn information, skills, and concepts at the same rate. This is one indicator of student readiness.

Students in a classroom have had varied life experiences and therefore bring different levels of readiness for any given topic. If, for example, a child grew up near a large lake, she probably learned to fish and swim at an early age. She may also have learned to water ski. If, however, a child grew up in a city, he learned how to take a bus or subway, visited large museums, and is accustomed to having many shops and restaurants from which to select. These two children have different life experiences, which is another element of student readiness. A teacher should structure lesson plans to include aspects of life to help students learn why they are learning the information, and how to transfer and use that information in their own lives.

Student Interest

It is important to engage learners at the beginning of a lesson. Two powerful motivators to get students engaged are **student interest** and **student choice** (Bess, 1997; Brandt, 1998). Students who are interested in a topic are more likely to learn the new content or skill. A teacher tries to identify the interests of the students and incorporate those interests when possible. In addition, teachers try to create interest in new topics by providing interesting learning experiences and environments. When students have a choice about what or how they demonstrate what they have learned, they are more likely to be more engaged. And academically engaged children usually have higher academic achievement. At least one research study has found that children given more opportunity to make choices about schoolwork score higher on standardized tests (Boggiano, 1992).

How might a teacher implement student interest? One teacher, Mr. Charles, is planning a series of lessons about writing paragraphs. He knows that all the children in his class love animals. He will be sure to incorporate this interest during his instruction and in the topic selections he provides for the children. Mr. Charles knows that all the children don't like the same types of animals, so he'll fill the room with pictures and books about all types of animals. Perhaps he will even decorate his room to look like a zoo or a tropical rain forest. He could place simple paragraphs, similar to the type he will expect the children to write, beside some animals around the room. Other animal pictures would not have paragraphs next to them. They would be placed there by the children who choose to write about them. In these ways, Mr. Charles is building on a known interest as well as creating an inviting environment that will encourage children to express their thoughts through writing. By allowing each child to select his or her own animal to write about, Mr. Charles is empowering the children and further encouraging student engagement. Therefore student success is more likely.

LEARNING PROFILE

Learning profile refers to the way in which individuals prefer to learn. The **learning environment** and **intelligence preference** are two of many factors that can contribute to a student's learning profile. An effective teacher knows how his or her students prefer to learn and plans lessons that incorporate the opportunity to use those options during the learning process.

Intelligence Preference

Intelligence preference (see Figure 6.3) refers to the various brain-based preferences everyone has for learning. Although several scholars have studied intelligence, perhaps the theory most often referred to in the American school setting is Howard Gardner's theory of Multiple

---

INTELLIGENCE PREFERENCE

Gardner's Theory of Multiple Intelligences

Verbal/Linguistic—can express oneself through spoken and written language.

Logical/Mathematical—can easily reason, detect patterns, and think logically.

Musical—is skilled in performance, composition, and appreciation of musical patterns, pitches, tones, and rhythms.

Bodily/Kinesthetic—uses the whole body or parts to solve problems.

Visual/Spatial—recognizes and uses patterns of small and large spaces.

Interpersonal—understands and works well with others.

Intrapersonal—understands self and prefers to work alone.

Naturalist—can recognize and categorize environmental features.

FIGURE 6.3 Intelligence Preference

(Adapted by M. K. Schoenfeldt from Gardner, 1993.)

Intelligences. Gardner (1993) suggests that learners have varying strengths in one or more of intelligences that he lists as verbal/ linguistic, logical/mathematical, visual/spatial, musical/rhythmic, bodily/kinesthetic, interpersonal, intrapersonal, and naturalist. A teacher can try to teach the content in ways that appeal to more than one of the intelligences and try to incorporate each at least once during a week.

In developing a lesson about the four seasons, Ms. Shire made a special effort to incorporate as many of the intelligences as she could. The topic itself appealed to the Naturalists. She designed her lesson plan to include some small group activities to appeal to the Interpersonal learners, a neighborhood walk to look for seasonal signs for the Bodily-Kinesthetic learners, taught songs with seasonal themes for the Musical learners, decorated the room with lots of visuals of all four seasons for the Visual learners, and had students journal about their walk to appeal to both the Verbal-Linguistic and Intrapersonal learners. This topic lends itself quite easily to all types of intelligences. All lesson topics will not. But most can incorporate more than one intelligence preference.

Environment

Some students prefer a quiet room, while others like to have music playing in the background. Some students learn best when instruction is oral, while others prefer visuals, and still others need tactile experiences. Some students work productively at their desks;

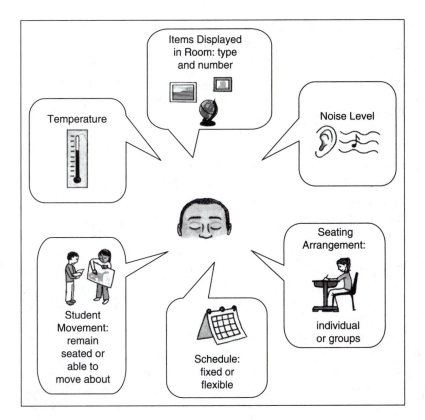

FIGURE 6.4 Room Environmental Elements to Consider

others work more efficiently sitting or lying on the floor. The amount of light and the temperature of the room can also affect learners in different ways. Although a teacher cannot accommodate all these preferences at all times, it *is* possible for the teacher to create different environments in different sections of the room, or on different days or times of the day (see Figure 6.4).

In a self-contained elementary classroom, teachers often set up zones or areas for various functions to create a welcoming environment and to accommodate the many interests of the students. Mr. David, for example, has a reading area with child-sized rocking chairs and interesting books to encourage free-time reading. He also has an area for listening to music, complete with MP3 and CD players, earphones, and a selection of CDs. In another area, Mr. David sets out a collection of art supplies, including markers, crayons, paper, scissors, and glue. And the computer area, complete with five laptops with headphones, educational software, and Internet connection, is yet another popular zone. He works in a time each day for students to select an area in which to work.

Another elementary teacher, Ms. Berry, tries to accommodate the different learners in her elementary room by setting up various informal learning areas of the room. One is a comfortable reading area complete with beanbag chairs and a well-stocked bookshelf nearby; another offers round tables for collaborative work. She allows students to move to those locations when working on assignments rather than staying at their desks. Ms. Berry also provides a couple of CD players with earphones and a selection of CDs for students to use while they study. She reports that her efforts have been successful because her students have become more productive in class and less disruptive.

Most middle school and high school classrooms accommodate many groups of students in the course of a school day. It is still important for teachers to try to create a welcoming environment. In Ms. Barlow's middle school social studies classroom, she displays student work on one bulletin board. Another is dedicated to correspondence that arrives from the Flat Stanley project (Hubert, 1995; Brown, 2004). Students eagerly check that bulletin board to see if "their" Stanley's companions have sent a postcard. Nearby is a map with small sticky dots attached to all the spots from which correspondence has come. And the board above the computer zone contains copies of e-mails from the 50 states e-Pal project (Zolt & DiScipio, 2007).

In his high school English classroom, Mr. Edwards has posters displaying lyrics to selected popular and historically significant songs alongside poetry from American poets past and present. Nearby is a bulletin board with song lyrics and poetry created by his students juxtaposed with their famous counterpart that served as inspiration. Near the computer station are various reference sources that are used during student research projects and when questions arise during class. Mr. David, Ms. Berry, Ms. Barlow, and Mr. Edwards are all trying to make their rooms inviting places where learning can occur. Each has taken their students' interests into consideration when designing the layout and design elements of their rooms.

ORGANIZATIONAL CONSIDERATIONS

Teachers who differentiate instruction in an effort to meet the diverse academic needs of their students use a variety of organizational ideas. These include, but are certainly not limited to a variety of learning centers, contracts, curriculum compacting, anchor activities, and learning buddies (partnerships). **Learning centers** offer learning activities and experiences in various locations around the room that can be completed alone, in pairs, or in small groups depending on how the teacher sets up each center. Each center focuses on one subject or content area (math, science, and writing) but provides multiple ways in which to interact with the lesson's content. Children may rotate among all the centers each day or each week. Sometimes there are tiered activities at each center, and children are assigned tasks that meet their individual needs. Some teachers use learning contracts with students. The

learning contract outlines what the child is to learn, how to go about gathering information, how to demonstrate learning, and includes a timeline for completion. Learning contracts accommodate student interest and choice.

Some children move quickly through a lesson's content. Teachers who differentiate might consider using **curriculum compacting.** Students who can competently pass a lesson's posttest prior to the beginning of a lesson are allowed to "compact out" of that lesson. They are allowed to explore *related* topics of their own choosing with their teacher's approval. The teacher recognizes that the students do not need to practice something they already fully understand. Some teachers are hesitant to use curriculum compacting. They believe that even if a child understands the content, extra practice is a good thing.

Suppose that you have just finished writing your lesson plan. Your principal walks in, reads it carefully, and comments on what a fine lesson plan it is. Then he tells you to write another one because "practice makes perfect" and "you can never get too much practice." Or suppose you just finished washing, drying, and folding the laundry. Your roommate walks in and thanks you for doing hers, too. But then she says that you should do it all over again because you need the practice. Both are ridiculous situations, right? Well, children who have already mastered a lesson's content don't necessarily need to practice again either, and they might view a teacher's request to solve 10 more math problems just as you would the principal's and roommate's requests. "I've already done a thorough job. Let me try something new." Try to remember these ridiculous stories when you have students who are capable of compacting out.

All students do not complete tasks at the same rate, and so there is always time when some students are still working and others are looking for something to do. **Anchor activities** are optional tasks for students to try after assigned work is completed, provided that the work is completed satisfactorily. These options are meant to be completed independently and might include journaling, problem-solving activities, reading, using manipulatives like tangrams, and using computer software programs. These activities can also be used for most of the class while the teacher meets with a small group.

UNDERSTANDING CONTENT

Several characteristics of a competent classroom teacher were identified by Jarolimek, Foster, and Kellough (2005). The first of these competencies, which also corresponds to INTASC Principle 1, is "the teacher is knowledgeable about the subject matter content expected to be taught" (p. 59). The second in their list refers to a teacher being an "educational broker." This term is defined as a teacher's ability to know where and how to find information about the content the teacher is expected to teach. It isn't possible for any elementary teacher to know everything about every lesson in every subject area she will be expected to teach. But every teacher *is* expected to become knowledgeable before attempting to teach specific content.

When writing a lesson plan, a teacher identifies a topic and finds relevant academic standards that help bring focus to what should be taught in order to create the lesson's goals and objectives. The next step is becoming informed. The old saying "You can't teach what you yourself don't know" applies. The quote applies equally to all teachers. An inexperienced teacher won't have prior experience in knowing what to teach or how to teach a particular topic. Experienced teachers want and need to keep current. So, all teachers at this point in the development of a lesson seek out sources of information to help them prepare.

A teacher seeks two basic types of sources: informational and instructional. **Informational** sources provide a teacher with topic-related content knowledge. **Instructional sources** provide a teacher with pedagogical ideas about how to teach a particular topic to a certain age of student. It is important to remember that these are not lesson materials that will be used with students during the lesson, but rather are "adult-level" teacher sources.

Informational

Let's say that a teacher is planning to teach second graders about disease transmission. That teacher needs to know the latest information on how various common childhood diseases are transmitted as well as how to prevent the spread of those diseases. Reputable Internet sites can be a good place to start because search engines speed up the research process. Reading through the teacher's edition of the health or science textbook can also provide some information.

Good informational sources can be found at local, school, and university libraries, too. Librarians and media specialists can be especially helpful in recommending certain sources. When searching for content information, it is important to find at least two sources. If there is disagreement between the two sources, it becomes necessary to find a third. The third source should agree with one of your other sources. Then once two sources that agree are found, it is necessary to find a third to verify accuracy.

It is important for a teacher to know more about the topic than what he plans to share with the students. Sometimes this extra information is referred to as "storeroom" knowledge. A teacher stores away more information than he thinks he'll need to teach the lesson. He can go to the "storeroom" during instruction for additional information if students ask questions beyond the scope of the planned lesson content. The better a teacher knows the lesson's content, the more confident he will be, and the more meaningful he can make the content for the students.

This is a good time to add a warning: Do not under any circumstances make up information during a lesson hoping that it is accurate. If you are not absolutely sure that information you are about to share is completely accurate, say, "That is a good question. Let's look that up together." Teachers must try to teach information correctly the first time, or otherwise they can end up spending a lot of time trying to correct errors and misconceptions. If students learn erroneous information, and the errors are not corrected quickly, those errors can become learned, habitual, and automatic and are then much harder to "unlearn" (Sousa, 2001; Personal Best Systems, 2005).

Instructional

The mediocre teacher tells. The good teacher explains. The superior teacher demonstrates. The great teacher inspires.
—William Arthur Ward

Becoming well informed about the content of a lesson is only half of the necessary preparation. It isn't enough to be well informed about disease transmission, for example, even with extra "storeroom" knowledge. It is also necessary to find sources that recommend ways to teach the content to a particular group of students. INTASC Principle 4 states, "The professional educator understands and uses a variety of instructional strategies to encourage students' development of critical thinking, problem solving and performance skills" (Council of Chief State School Officers, 1992). In addition, teachers must keep in mind the specific needs of the children in the classroom while preparing the lesson. This correlates with INTASC principal 2, "The professional educator understands how children learn and develop and can provide learning opportunities that support their intellectual, social, and personal development" (Council of Chief State School Officers, 1992).

A second-grade lesson on disease transmission is quite different from one taught in a high school health or science lesson. It is

 Reality Check

Question: Where do you find information sources for your lesson?

I would definitely begin by looking at the classroom text if there is one. At least I would know what content to be looking for. Then I'd hop online, check out the local library or professional development resource lab.

Amanda Williams
Kindergarten

important to keep developmental appropriateness in mind. The teacher's edition is a starting point because it was developed and written for a specific grade level. The Internet can also be helpful as long as the sites used are reputable. There are many excellent "teacher Web sites" that provide lesson plan ideas, usually arranged by grade level and topic. Teacher magazines and activity books can provide ideas. Asking other teachers is a good idea. It is not necessary to reinvent the wheel. Many teachers have taught the same content to the selected grade level. Use their knowledge and experience. Keep in mind the quote by William Arthur Ward from the beginning of this section while you select your instructional sources. Look for instructional ideas that will help you inspire your learners. Think back to your own school days to remember teachers who inspired you to learn. What did they do that made lessons memorable?

While searching for instructional sources, it is important to keep in mind that certain instructional strategies or methods are more effective than others in positively affecting student achievement and fostering long-term retention of information. Marzano, Pickering, and Pollock (2001) list identifying similarities and differences, summarizing, nonlinguistic representations, cooperative learning, and generating and testing hypotheses as being among the most effective strategies. In the 1960s, the National Training Laboratories (now the NTL Institute) devised a "learning pyramid," which was based on earlier work by Edgar Dale. Both showed students' long-term retention rates tied to various classroom instructional practices. Dale called his rendering the Cone of Experience and describes it "as a metaphor for concept development" (Seels, 1997, p. 2). Dale (1969) visualized educational experiences in concrete to abstract layers within the cone. The revisualization in Figure 6.5 shows the same information. Note that the effectiveness of the instructional methods are not cumulative. That is, if a teacher has students read and listen to a lecture, the average retention rate is not 15%. Lecture is the least effective instructional method for long-term retention, which closely aligns with Ward's quote about mediocre teachers who "tell." As you look down the layers in Figure 6.5, you note that each layer requires more active student involvement.

While developing a second-grade disease transmission lesson, a teacher might decide to teach the new content through demonstration, visuals, and cooperative groups. The teacher could first show visuals and demonstrate disease transmission through sneezing, coughing, and touching. Then the students, in their cooperative groups, could create and perform for the class their own original demonstrations that depict specific instances of disease transmission that might occur in the school or classroom setting. In this way, the teacher is using several of the ideas from both Marzano's reporting and the learning experiences identified in Figure 6.5. In addition, most teachers talk with other teachers.

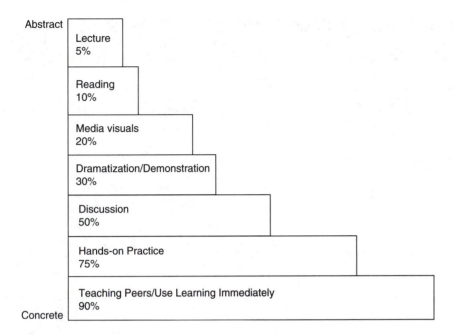

FIGURE 6.5 Learning Experiences, Abstract to Concrete
(Adapted by D. E. Salsbury from Dale's Cone of Experience, 1969.)

I hear and I forget. I see and I remember. I do and I understand.
—Confucius

It is important to write down the informational and instructional sources gathered. An annotated bibliography is most helpful. The annotation provides a brief explanation of where the source was found and how it was useful. In fact, the next time the lesson is taught, a lesson plan bibliography provides a starting point for preparing to teach. The bibliography allows a teacher to refer to previously used sources of information before beginning a check for updates in information and new teaching ideas.

In fact, many experienced teachers keep files, paper or digital, of past lessons. In the file, teachers place copies of content-related

 ## *Reality Check*

Question: Where do you find instructional strategy ideas?

The best thing I ever did as a beginning teacher was when I spent a good amount of time talking to other second-grade teachers that were experienced and those who loved their job! It really got me excited and gave me a clear understanding of what second-grade children are like.

Alyson Woodruff
Brooks School Elementary
Second grade

Reality Check

Question: Is it important to keep files of lesson plan resources?

My first year of teaching was all about survival. I worked so hard to make sure my kids had the best lessons I could give them, while trying to balance the organization and responsibilities of a first-year teacher.

When I went back to teach the same subjects a year or two later, I found myself often wishing that I had written out a little more detail in my plans. Sometimes I would wonder what application activity I had given them after a lesson, and other times, I had the name of a worksheet written down, but no idea where that page came from! I never realized how quickly we can forget things, but I do now! It's even more challenging for me as a multiage teacher because I cannot reuse activities two years in a row. So to try and remember an activity that was done two years ago is not always the best way. I've tried to be a little more detailed with my planning, in order to save me some time in the future!

Carrie Smith
Prairie Vista Elementary School
Fourth- and fifth-grade multiage

information, lists of teaching ideas, suggestions for materials to use with the children, and copies of the original and subsequently developed lesson plans. It can be very frustrating and time consuming to try to find that "excellent source" used before. If it is written down and filed, much time can be saved and frustration avoided.

IN SUMMARY

Teachers can't teach what they themselves don't know. It isn't possible for any elementary teacher to know everything about every lesson in every subject area she will be expected to teach. But every teacher *is* expected to become knowledgeable before attempting to teach specific content. Becoming well informed about the content of a lesson is only half of the necessary preparation. It is also necessary to find sources that recommend ways to teach the content to a particular group of students.

 UNIT CONNECTION

There is no difference in the need to collect informational and instructional sources to prepare either a stand-alone lesson or lessons that are part of a unit. Both types of planning require the teacher to gather content and instructional information. It is always important to become knowledgeable in content, the *what to teach*, and instructional, the *how to teach*, techniques.

YOUR TURN

 ACTIVITY 1: Identify Your Informational Sources

INTASC Principles 1 and 7

Directions: You have identified a topic for your lesson. You have identified relevant academic standards and written an objective. Now you need to become informed enough to be able to teach the lesson by locating two or more informational sources that tell you *what to teach.*

1. Find at least two informational sources. These help you determine your lesson's content. These are *teacher* informational sources; sources that help *you* review the content of your lesson.

2. Record complete bibliographical information for each source.

3. Provide a brief explanation of how the resource was helpful to you in preparing to teach the lesson's content.

4. Tell the location (i.e., school library, Web site URL) of each source so that you can find it again later.

 ACTIVITY 2: Identify Your Instructional Sources

INTASC Principles 2, 3, 4, and 7

Directions: You have identified a topic for your lesson. You have identified relevant academic standards and written an objective. Now you need to become informed enough to be able to teach the lesson by locating two or more instructional sources that tell you *how to teach* the content to your students.

1. Find at least two instructional sources.

2. Give the complete bibliographical information for each source.

3. Provide a brief explanation of how the resource was helpful to you in preparing to teach the lesson to your grade-level students. Identify the strategies you will design into your lesson (i.e., cooperative learning, finding similarities and differences, role playing).

4. Tell the location of each source so that you can find it again later.

ACTIVITY 3: Creating a Lesson Plan Annotated Bibliography

INTASC Principles 1, 2, 3, 4, and 7

Directions: After you have located the informational and instructional resources for your lesson, complete the following form. Start a lesson file and include a copy of this information. Later you can add your completed lesson plan(s) and materials list to this same file. The next time you teach this topic, you will only need to make modifications rather than start all over.

ANNOTATED LESSON PLAN BIBLIOGRAPHY

Your Name:

Lesson Topic:

Grade Level:

Subject(s)/Discipline(s) (e.g., math, language arts, etc):

Academic Standard(s):

Informational Sources:

Instructional Sources:

Sample Lesson Plan Annotated Bibliography

Lesson Topic: Functions of Government

Grade Level: Second

Subject/Discipline: Social Studies

(National) Academic Standard: #6—Power, Authority, and Governance (National Council for the Social Studies, 1994)

Informational Resources:

1. Armstrong, R. (2002). *Covering government: A civics handbook for journalists.* Ames, IA: Iowa State Press.

   Covering Government provides information on federal, state, and local governmental structures. There is a fairly clear explanation of the division of the three governmental branches: legislative, executive, and judicial. The author describes a variety of events, though some are not appropriate topics for this lesson. There are overviews explaining the functions and rules of governmental branches.

   The information in *Covering Government* helped me create a diagram of the three governmental branches. We can refer to the diagram during discussion and practice activities.

2. Indiana Chamber of Commerce. (2001). *Here is your Indiana government.* Indianapolis, IN: Indiana Chamber of Commerce.

Here Is Your Indiana Government furthered my knowledge about local government by breaking it down into units consisting of counties, townships, and cities. It then described the responsibilities of each unit, the leaders of each unit, and their duties.

I plan to write the information from the resource on different cards, then create a type of schematic puzzle diagramming the relationships of a city to a township and a township to a county. Students can use the cards for showing other relationships between governmental units.

Instructional (Pedagogy) Resources:

1. U.S. Government Printing Office. (2004). *GPO access.* Retrieved 2007 from http://www.gpoaccess.gov/about/index.html.

The Web site provides free, official information from the federal government. It contains links to the National Archives and other federal documents, as well as to an online governmental bookstore. There also a link to *Ben's Guide to U.S. Government for Kids.* In particular, on the Branches of Government Web page there is a diagram showing the basic structure of the three branches of government.

The Web site has a variety of primary sources, yet they could not be used at this grade level. I plan to obtain pictures of government buildings and people for transparencies and flashcards. I could use the transparencies to show the relationships of different governmental agencies, then integrate the children's Web site as a practice activity for the students.

2. Banks, J., Boehm, R., Colleary, K., Contreras, G., Goodwin, A. L., & McFarland, M. (2003). *Social studies: Our communities* (Teacher's ed.). New York: Macmillan/McGraw-Hill.

The teacher's edition provides background information about community government. The explanations will be helpful when describing what community government is to second graders. It also gives questions I can ask the children about local government, such as, "Who usually leads community government?"

There are many different instructional strategies to use for activating prior knowledge through a variety of activities. A flowchart could explain the relationships of the government jobs.

 ACTIVITY 4: Collaboration

INTASC Principle 10

Directions: Work with two or three other people who are also completing these activities.

1. Share your instructional sources aloud with each other.

   • How do they fit with your ideas about teaching and learning?
   • How do they meet individual differences of your students?
   • How will they motivate and interest your students?

2. Tell where you were able to find the resources you needed. Was the Internet most helpful? Were teacher's editions more helpful?

 ACTIVITY 5: Reflection

INTASC Principle 9

Directions: Write a brief response to the following questions.

1. What decisions did you have to make to create your lesson plan's bibliography?

2. Did the process of creating this bibliography change your view of the teaching profession? Why or why not?

3. Do you have a more clear understanding of the direction your lesson will take? Why or why not?

REFERENCES

Bess, J. (1997). *Teaching well and liking it: Motivating faculty to teach effectively.* Baltimore, MD: The Johns Hopkins University Press.

Boggiano, B. K. (1992). Helplessness deficits in students: The role of motivational orientation. *Motivation and Emotion, 16, 278–280.*

Brandt, R. (1998). *Powerful learning.* Alexandria, VA: Association for Supervision and Curriculum Development.

Brown, J. (2004). *Flat Stanley [40th anniversary ed.].* New York: Harper Collins.

Council of Chief State School Officers. (1992). *Model standards for beginning teacher licensing and development: A resource for state dialogue [INTASC standards].* Washington, D.C.: Author. Retrieved April, 2006, from http://www.ccsso.org/content/pdfs/corestrd.pdf

Dale, E. (1969). *Audiovisual methods in teaching* (3rd ed.). New York: Holt, Rinehart and Winston.

Davidson Institute for Talent Development. (2003). *Does no child left behind mean no child can get ahead?* [Archived News Releases 2003]. Retrieved April 23, 2006, from http://www.presskit.ditd.org/2003_News_Releases/pr_2003_Indianapolis-NAGC.html

Gardner, H. (1993). *Frames of mind: The theory of multiple intelligences.* New York, NY: Basic Books.

Jarolimek, J., Foster, C., & Kellough, R. (2005). *Teaching and learning in the elementary school* (8th ed.). Upper Saddle River, NJ: Merrill/Prentice Hall.

Kiernan, L. (Producer). (1997). *Differentiating instruction* [Videotape interview with C. A. Tomlinson]. Alexandria, VA: Association for Supervision and Curriculum Development.

King-Sears, M. E. (2001). Three steps for gaining access to the general education curriculum for learners with disabilities. *Intervention in School & Clinic, 37*(2), 67–76.

Malone, T. (2004). *What can happen to bored gifted students?* Retrieved April 23, 2006, from http://www.susanohanian.org/show special_news.html?id=269.

Marzano, R., Pickering, D., & Pollock, J. (2001). *Classroom instruction that works: Research-based strategies for increasing student achievement.* Alexandria, VA: Association for Supervision and Curriculum Development.

National Association for Gifted Children (NAGC). (2006). *What is gifted? Current definitions.* Retrieved April 23, 2006, from http://www.nagc.org/index.aspx?id=574&ir.

Personal Best Systems. (2005). *Habit pattern correction for better learning transfer.* Queensland, Australia: Author.

Sanders, W., & Rivers, J. (1996). *Cumulative and residual effects of teachers on future student academic achievement.* Knoxville, TN: University of Tennessee Value-Added Research and Assessment Center.

Seels, B. (1997). The relationship of media and ISD theory: The unrealized promise of Dale's "Cone of Experience". In *Proceedings of Selected Research and Development Presentations at the 19th National Convention of the Association for Educational Communications and Technology.* Albuquerque, NM. (ERIC Document Reproduction Service No. ED 409869)

Sousa, D. (2001). *How the brain learns* (2nd ed.). Thousand Oaks, CA: Corwin Press.

Tomlinson, C. A. (2001). *How to differentiate instruction in mixed ability classrooms* (2nd ed.). Alexandria, VA: Association for Supervision and Curriculum Development.

U. S. Department of Education. (2007). *Ed.gov:* No Child Left Behind. Retrieved January, 2007, from No Child Left Behind Web site: http://www.ed.gov/nclb/landing.jhtml.

Zolt, N., & DiScipio, T. (2007). *ePals: Global community.* Retrieved August, 2007, from ePals site: http://www.epalscorp.com/about/index. html.

Selecting Lesson Materials

Objective: Select lesson materials.

1.1 Identify 1 relevant piece of literature.
1.2 Identify 2 relevant visual aids.
1.3 Identify 1 relevant activity and its materials.

Using our road trip analogy, materials are the items we will pack and intend to use throughout the trip (Figure 7.1, p. 100).

Relevant INTASC Principles: #1, #2, #3, #4, #5, #6, #7, #8, #9 (See inside back cover of this book for complete list.)

THE NEXT STEP: SELECTING MATERIALS

So far in planning your lesson, you have selected a curricular-related topic, established a standards connection to the topic, written both a lesson goal and objective, researched and recorded content and pedagogical sources, and decided on the method of assessing your students' learning. The next step is to select the materials that you will use with students during the lesson.

Before a trip begins, travelers pack their bags. The items they pack correspond to their interests and expectations of the trip. The travelers may want to stop and see the sights in the nearest town, which could require a guidebook, money for shopping, comfortable clothing, and walking shoes for sightseeing. On our pretend ski trip to Colorado, our travelers will also need to pack ski gear.

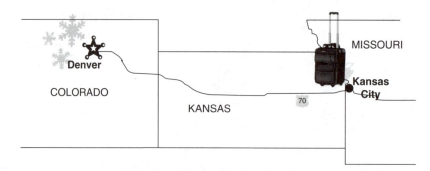

FIGURE 7.1   Packing for the Road Trip

MATERIALS DEFINED

Materials are any item, tool, or piece of equipment used to support the lesson before, during, or after instruction. Not to be confused with informational and instructional resources gathered in chapter 6, materials are incorporated during a lesson to attract the attention of the learners and to strengthen the students' connection and understanding of the lesson's content. The most basic materials in most classrooms are paper, pencils, chalk, chalkboard, and books.

Materials are used by teachers during instruction and by the students during guided and independent practice of the new information. Materials can be **visual aids** such as posters, maps, videos, or photos; **media equipment** such as computers, a video camera, CD/DVD player, webcam, or digital camera; **tools** such as rulers, calculators, and measuring cups; **realia** such as birds' nests, rocks, live animals, and musical instruments; **print sources** such as books, magazines, Web sites, or song lyrics; or **manipulatives** such as unifix cubes, geoboards, counters, and tangrams.

Realia refers to three-dimensional objects from real life, whether man-made (artifacts, tools, utensils, etc.) or naturally occurring (specimens, samples, etc.). In the beginning of a lesson about percussion instruments, to gain students' interest, a teacher might pass around a triangle, a bongo drum, and cymbals. These are examples of realia.

If you look at the list of material types, you'll probably notice that some lesson materials can fall into more than one category. An Internet Web site, for example, might be used as a print source for the text it contains and for the many visuals in both still photo and video clip formats. Computers can be used by teachers or students to demonstrate how to find information and to create a word document or PowerPoint presentation.

WHAT RESEARCH SAYS

Well-chosen materials support the lesson topic, encourage student engagement, and stimulate learning. Understanding what researchers have discovered about various types of materials and their impact on student achievement, retention of learning, and engagement with content is important. Expert teachers search out effective materials for each lesson.

Brain Research

Brain research stresses the impact of sight, touch, hearing, taste, and smell to student learning experiences (Sousa, 2001). Hearing, sight, and touch contribute the most to new learning. It becomes clear, then, why realia can play such an important role. Learners touch and see them and hear the teacher's explanation. Other types of visual aids are important as well because they stimulate learning through the sense of sight (Sousa, 2001). If the visual aid can also be touched (a model), smelled (a flower), or tasted (any food item), more brain connections can be made. By stimulating several senses during learning, more connections to the content are made in students' brains. These connections provide multiple paths for later recall of the information (Willis, 2006). When selecting lesson materials, then, teachers should consider the impact of the senses in initial learning and later recall.

Brain research also tells us that a person's brain is constantly seeking novelty (Sousa, 2001). By providing students with new experiences, teachers are attempting to increase student learning. Reading and writing are expected lesson activities. Role playing, singing, conducting experiments, or taking field trips may not be as common, so they provide novelty for students. In addition, they most likely involve the use of multiple senses, again increasing the chance for long-term retention of the lesson's content. Well-selected lesson activities thus can serve a vital function.

 **TECHNOLOGY IN EDUCATION**

An outstanding site for **locating materials,** "Thinkfinity" allows you to search by topic, grade level, and subject area; go to http://www.marcopoloeducation.org/, then select Student Materials Index under the heading of Teacher Resources.

For **culturally responsive materials,** go to http://www.ncela.gwu.edu/practice/tolerance/6_web.htm.

For **printable templates** (calendars, graphic organizers, charts, etc.), go to http://www.educationworld.com/tools_templates/index.shtml.

For printable and online **manipulatives,** go to http://nlvm.usu.edu/en/nav/vlibrary.html.

Literacy

Teachers serve as models of correct language usage in all lessons regardless of the lesson's content area. They are mindful, too, that students are continuously developing their own literacy skills. "Children and adults use language as a tool for getting needs met, for thinking, for solving problems, and for sharing ideas and emotions" (Reutzel & Cooter, 2000, p.51). Teachers can model the significance of written language as an important tool for documenting and communicating information by incorporating print sources into every lesson. It is therefore advisable to include some type of literature or print materials in every lesson.

Technology as an Instructional Tool

Students today are considered "digital natives" (Prensky, 2001). They have spent their entire lives surrounded by and using computers, videogames, videocams, and cell phones. Using this technology has conditioned their brains to accept information quickly. These digital natives often have a greater understanding of current technological capabilities than do their teachers (McHale, 2005). But does research support the integration of technology into classrooms? Is it worth the time for teachers to learn how to use these new materials?

High school students at a technology-integrated school demonstrated average increases of 94 points in combined SAT I performance over students who participated in the traditional school experience (Bain & Ross, 2000). In a study in Virginia, the use of digital video clips to supplement instruction in third- and eighth-grade classes resulted in increased student achievement (Boster, Meyer, Roberto, & Inge, 2002). Upper elementary students who used a software collaboration tool called Computer Supported Intentional Learning Environment (CSILE) performed better on standardized tests in reading, language, and vocabulary than students who did not use the software. They also scored better on tests of depth of understanding, multiple perspectives, and independent thought (Scardamalia & Bereiter, 1996). Teachers

 ## *Reality Check*

Question: Do you consider your students when you select lesson materials?

As an art teacher, I try to remind myself, no matter how much of a headache I may be creating for myself as the teacher by coming up with messy lessons, the students will probably love it. Students retain what you want them to learn if they are doing something they truly enjoy. I try to incorporate different mediums, so students will be able to have a chance to have lots of favorites!

Jill Carson-Coen
Art Teacher
Harris and Weston Elementary Schools

 **TECHNOLOGY IN EDUCATION**

Are you a "digital native"? Take a quiz to find out! Go to: http://coe.sdsu.edu/eet/.

To find research on the effectiveness of **integrating technology,** go to the Center for Applied Research in Educational Technology at http://caret.iste.org/index.cfm?useaction=topics.

To view the **Technology Standards for Students [NET-S],** go to http://www.iste.org/inhouse/Nets/cnets/index.html.

who are high-level technology users, in terms of frequency and extent of use, significantly increased their students' academic achievement, much more so than teachers who were low-level users (Middleton & Murray, 1999).

Other research on the effectiveness of integrating technology into classrooms focused on student motivation to learn. Underwood and Brown (1997) found that students were more motivated to work when allowed to use computers because of the ease of correcting errors in writing and the ability to work at their own pace. Cotton (1992) found computer-assisted instruction resulted in improved student attitudes toward themselves as learners. Cotton also found that students who use technology at school have a better school attendance rate, increased time on task, and better behavior.

In 176 studies, Sivin-Kachala and Bialo (1994) found students' attitudes toward learning consistently increased in a technology-rich environment. Students and teachers both reported a positive change in student motivation for class assignments when multimedia was incorporated into classroom instruction (Cradler & Cradler, 1999). With all of this evidence, and there is much more available, it becomes imperative that today's teachers keep abreast of new technologies and learn how they can be used to engage their learners.

MEETING THE NEEDS OF ALL LEARNERS

A teacher makes selections of materials based on students' readiness, interests, and learning styles, and chooses materials that are culturally responsive. Considerations of how the materials will be used during instruction based on students' readiness can be represented within a concrete-to-abstract continuum (Burden & Byrd, 2003). Students who are less familiar with a lesson's content need more concrete materials. They need to use as many of their senses as possible to explore the new information. Realistic representations of actual items fall in the middle of the continuum and can be used once students have some grasp of the content and to review. At the abstract

Concrete		Abstract
←— —→		
realia, manipulatives	photos, visual aids	text, symbols

FIGURE 7.2   Concrete-to-Abstract Continuum

(Adapted by M. K. Schoenfeldt from Burden and Byrd, 2003.)

end are materials that are more symbolic representations of the content. Refer to Figure 7.2.

If students are learning about the three rock types in science, for example, the best lesson "materials" would be examples of each type, and teachers could bring in samples. It may be practical to take a field trip to a museum or quarry to see various rocks. Once students are familiar with the characteristics of the rock types, photos and diagrams can be used to reinforce and review the content. Finally, students could use text-based materials like an encyclopedia, their science textbook, or a nonfiction book to find more information.

If students are studying addition in math, they could first explore combining two amounts using manipulatives. Then they could look at pictorial representations of sets, and lastly, they would be ready to see the number problem. In both examples, the materials selected to begin the lesson were concrete. As students became more familiar with the content, the materials selected were more and more abstract. All students are not ready to move along the concrete-to-abstract continuum at the same rate. In fact, many students will remain at the concrete end for quite some time. A teacher will know through observation and questioning when students are ready to use less concrete materials.

Teachers know students are more engaged in the learning process if there is some connection between the content scheduled to be taught and the students' interests. When students are interested in the lesson topic and find the information meaningful, they are more likely to participate in the learning experiences. If the materials are interesting, the students are much more likely to be engaged and learning (Tomlinson, 2001). If a teacher is designing a lesson about technological advances, for example, students could choose which type most interests them. The teacher could collect materials to support those interests.

Teacher decisions for choosing which type of materials best support student learning are influenced by the students' **learning styles,** as defined in chapter 6, by the use of Gardner's theory of Multiple Intelligences (Armstrong, 2003; Gardner, 1999). Rather than identify learning style preferences of *each* student, most teachers incorporate a variety of instructional strategies and materials to suit several intelligences throughout a single lesson. The rule of thumb is to include materials and activities that meet the needs of two or more learning styles, because most students possess more than one type of intelligence to a greater or lesser degree. For example, in an eighth-grade lesson about character and plot, a teacher could assign a story (linguistic), have students act out scenes from the book (bodily-kinesthetic), and then ask students to draw a pictorial representation using a graphic organizer of the main character's traits (visual-spatial). Materials for the three parts of the lesson include one piece of literature (the story) and two activities that involve the student (acting, drawing).

Cultural Diversity

Materials should also reflect the cultural diversity of the students in the classroom, school building, and surrounding community. In the United States, all students belong to the American culture. But within any large culture are various subcultures. A **subculture** may be distinctive because of the age of its members, or by their race, ethnicity, class, or gender.

Most curricular materials supplied by a school district are expected to undergo an examination for cultural sensitivity before they are used with students. But many times, teachers select materials of their own. Some teachers spend considerable time, as well as their own money, to find materials to supplement classroom supplies. When setting up learning centers or stations, creating room displays, and selecting free-play items and books, a teacher should select materials that are culturally responsive. One teacher explained that she selected materials that provided a window and a mirror. A mirror reflects, and so each child should see materials in the classroom that reflect his or her culture. A window allows us to see into other places, so materials should allow all the students to "see into" other cultures.

Another teacher reported that she learned from parents at a parent-teacher conference that their daughter had come home declaring that she was now ready to be a boy. When asked why, the girl replied that in the stories the teacher read aloud, the boys had all the adventures and led exciting lives. The teacher quickly sought out and began including read-aloud stories with females in the leading roles. No child should be made to feel that they should become something else in order to fit in. They should at least occasionally "see themselves" in stories, photos, illustrations, and other lesson materials. The checklist in Figure 7.3 can assist teachers in selecting materials that are culturally responsive.

PRACTICAL CONSIDERATIONS IN USING MATERIALS

It is imperative for teachers to have all materials ready to use and located nearby before they begin instruction. Whether the teacher is providing instruction to a small group of students or the entire class, there should be enough materials for all students. In fact,

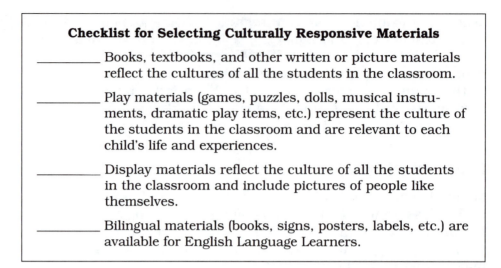

Checklist for Selecting Culturally Responsive Materials

_____ Books, textbooks, and other written or picture materials reflect the cultures of all the students in the classroom.

_____ Play materials (games, puzzles, dolls, musical instruments, dramatic play items, etc.) represent the culture of the students in the classroom and are relevant to each child's life and experiences.

_____ Display materials reflect the culture of all the students in the classroom and include pictures of people like themselves.

_____ Bilingual materials (books, signs, posters, labels, etc.) are available for English Language Learners.

FIGURE 7.3 Checklist for Selecting Culturally Responsive Materials (Adapted by M. K. Schoenfeldt from Hepburn, 2006.)

most experienced teachers have extra materials ready because they know that some materials may be lost or rendered useless during the lesson. A student may need a new copy of a handout because of a spill, need another pattern because he mistakenly cut it out incorrectly, or drop and break a test tube. Not having enough materials or not having them ready at the beginning of a lesson can cause delays in beginning the lesson. This "down time" can lead students to become restless and to begin acting up.

When using materials a teacher must make sure that every student has an equal chance to see and access them. If students are required to sit in place during instruction their view may be impaired by the distance between them and the visuals and realia. A teacher should walk around the room, gather students together nearer the objects, or hand the items around, if possible, so all learners have the opportunity to view them. If some piece of technology is used, then all students should have equitable access to it. Some teachers allow students who work above grade level to have access to more enriching and interesting materials. All students benefit from using such materials.

It is necessary for teachers to familiarize themselves with the function of the selected materials and equipment ahead of time. There is no excuse for teachers' lack of knowledge about equipment. Fumbling around, trying to get equipment to work or to gather materials, results in loss of valuable teaching time and distracts the teacher from being able to monitor student behavior. If a teacher plans to use a particular Web site, then she should preview it ahead of time and navigate through the various pages so that she is not surprised during the lesson by inappropriate content. Previewing materials allows a teacher to properly use the site rather than being unsure of how its content is organized or

Reality Check

Question: How do you select lesson materials?

As simple as it may sound, often I find ideas for materials in our teachers' manuals. They usually have suggested literature readings, hands-on activities, and visual aids. I either use the exact idea or activity or it acts as a springboard for other ideas. Our district is also a member of United Streaming, an online Web site that has great visuals for our lessons.

The literature books that we have used for years came mostly from our library, and (sets of books) were obtained from our own resourcefulness (grants, etc.). The twice-a-year collaborations that we have with our library resource person, our gifted teacher, and our grade-level team have also been instrumental in gathering material ideas, planning our lessons, and integrating our curriculum to meet the needs of all our students.

Alea Lafond
Fourth grade
Quail Run Elementary

relates to the lesson concepts. So, too, a teacher should preview videos, video clips, and DVDs before showing them in class. It is imperative that a teacher familiarize herself with the content in order to explain vocabulary terms, anticipate possible student misunderstanding of unfamiliar ideas, answer student questions, and make connections to students' lives and experiences.

Teachers must also select materials that are age and grade appropriate. Sharp pointed scissors may be fine in a fifth- or sixth-grade classroom, but not in a kindergarten classroom. Photos of the Nazi concentration camps could be appropriate in middle and high school classrooms, but would probably be inappropriate for use with elementary students. Teachers should check the age and grade levels identified on lesson materials to ensure they are accurately labeled. Books with reading levels that are too difficult will discourage active participation, while books with reading levels that are too easy may not provide enough interest. Videos that are identified for use with middle school students would be an inappropriate choice for use with second graders. The content of a book, video, or Web site should not be too difficult to understand nor too unsophisticated for the students. It is important to consider the age of the students when selecting all materials.

Sometimes, the subject area of the lesson points the teacher toward the selection of certain materials. Each academic area has particular materials associated with the discipline. Some materials, of course, overlap academic areas. Graphs, charts, and tables can be used in math, science, and social studies. In Figure 7.4, a few academic areas are identified with a short list of their associated materials. By no means are the discipline area lists all-inclusive. The national organizations that support each set of guidelines have Web sites with additional information about resources and materials. These Web sites are provided in the TiE of chapter 4.

Academic Area	Materials List
Social Studies: **Geography*** **History*** **Political Science/ Civics/Government*** **Economics*** **Sociology*** **Psychology*** **Anthropology** **Archaeology** **Law** **Philosophy** **Religion** *Generally accepted as elementary education discipline areas integrated under the title of social studies.	Maps/globes: world, state, & local; aerials; topographic; population Orientation equipment: flags; compass; punch devices Primary & secondary sources/documents: diaries; letters; interview notes; cemetery tombstones; census records; domestic & foreign newspapers; baseball cards; posters Political items: domestic & foreign flags; photographs; editorial cartoons Money: coins; banknotes; checkbook; currency from other countries Webs, charts, graphs, diagrams, flowcharts Textbooks, workbooks
Science	Skeletal representations: bones; animal skulls, rulers Weather instruments: thermometer, wind sock, rain gauge Webs, charts, graphs, diagrams, flowcharts Experiment supplies: test tubes; measuring cups; ramps; pulleys Microscopes, slides Posters: "Food Pyramid" Models: solar system; cells Textbooks, workbooks
Mathematics	Number charts Rulers, yardsticks, meter sticks, measuring cups Compass, protractor Webs, charts, graphs, diagrams, flowcharts Geoboard, base 10 blocks, unifix cubes, counters, money Textbooks, workbooks
Reading/Writing/ Language Arts	Fiction books Nonfiction books Poems Newspapers Felt/flannel boards Vocabulary cards Sentence strips Story starters Webs, charts, graphs, flowcharts Construction paper Textbooks, workbooks

FIGURE 7.4   Academic Area Materials List

IN SUMMARY

Teachers incorporate a variety of materials into lessons, including realia, print sources, visual aids, and technology. They select materials to support the lesson's content and objective and to meet the needs of the learners. Teachers consider students' readiness, interest, and learning styles when selecting some materials over others. Materials should be culturally responsive and age appropriate.

Teachers should prepare materials before beginning the lesson, prepare enough for all the students, and have extras in case they are needed. Teachers should be familiar with the content of each material and know how to properly use all equipment and technology. Well-chosen materials can engage the learners and encourage long-term retention of information by stimulating the brain through sensory-based stimuli. Considering research findings, lessons should include visual aids and literature or print sources, activities that provide novelty and actively involve learners, and integrate technology.

 ## UNIT CONNECTION

A unit is interdisciplinary, incorporating content, concepts, and skills from multiple subject areas. There will necessarily be many more materials used in a unit than in most stand-alone, single lessons. Figure 7.4 can serve as a reminder of the types of materials identified for various subject areas. In addition, keep in mind that the materials for a unit should include items from along the concrete-to-abstract continuum illustrated in Figure 7.2.

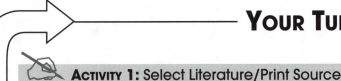 # YOUR TURN

ACTIVITY 1: Select Literature/Print Source

INTASC Principles 1, 2, 3, 5, 6, and 7

Directions: Complete the following tasks.

1. Identify *at least one* age-appropriate, topic-related piece of literature. This may be a fictional story, a nonfiction book, a poem, a news article, Web site, or song.

2. Copy complete bibliographic information for each piece of literature identified, including ISBN number if appropriate.

3. Write a brief explanation of how you plan to use this source in your lesson.

4. Write down the location where you found the source (e.g., library, Web site URL), so it can be found when you intend to use it again.

 ACTIVITY 2: Select an Activity and Its Corresponding Materials

INTASC Principles 1, 2, 3, 5, 6, and 7

Directions: Complete the following tasks.

1. Identify *at least one activity* that students can participate in during your lesson (e.g., conduct experiment, construct a model, role-play, create a collage, complete a WebQuest).

   a. Each activity should be age-appropriate and topic-related, and actively engage the learners.

   b. Each activity should provide students with opportunities to practice the content and skills you plan to teach during your lesson.

2. List the specific materials students will use during each activity (e.g., geoboard, calendar, Web site URL, newspaper).

3. Provide a brief explanation of how you plan to use each activity in your lesson.

4. Identify the location where you found the activity source.

 ACTIVITY 3: Select Visual Aids

INTASC Principles 1, 2, 3, 5, 6, and 7

Directions: Complete the following tasks.

1. List *at least two* specific, age-appropriate, topic-related visual aids that would support your lesson (e.g., diagram, model, chart, poster, photos).

2. Provide bibliographic information for each visual aid identified.

3. Write a brief explanation of how you plan to use the visual aid in your lesson.

4. Identify the location where you found the visual aid.

ACTIVITY 4: Create a Materials List

Directions: Complete the following blank template, listing the materials and media you chose to support your instruction and encourage student learning in your lesson plan. Add this to the file you started for this lesson.

MY LESSON'S MATERIALS LIST
BLANK TEMPLATE

Lesson Topic:

Grade Level:

Subject:

Academic Standard:

Lesson Objective:

Literature/Print Material:

Title:

Bibliographic citation:

   ISBN:

Summary:

Explanation:

Location:

Activity:

Student materials:

Teacher materials:

Bibliographic citation:

Explanation:

Location:

Visual Aids:

Visual Aid #1:

Type of visual:

Bibliographic citation:

Explanation:

Location:

Visual Aid #2:

Type of visual:

Bibliographic citation:

Explanation:

Location:

 ACTIVITY 5: Collaboration

INTASC Principle 10

Directions: Present information about your lesson materials.

1. Bring your selected materials to class. If any material is too cumbersome, bring a digital photograph of it.

2. In a small group, show each material (literature/print item, two visual aids, materials to be used by students in the lesson's activity) and briefly explain how you will use each in your lesson.

 ACTIVITY 6: Reflection

INTASC Principle 9

Directions: Write a brief response to the following questions.

1. What influenced your choices of materials?

2. Did you integrate technology? If so, how? If not, why not?

3. How did the process of collecting materials change your opinion of lesson planning?

REFERENCES

Armstrong, T. (2003). *The multiple intelligences of reading and writing: Making the words come alive.* Alexandria, VA: Association for Supervision and Curriculum Development.

Bain, A., & Ross, K. (2000). School reengineering and SAT-1 performance: A case study. *International Journal of Education Reform, 9*(2), 148–153.

Boster, F. J., Meyer, G. S., Roberto, A. J., & Inge, C. C. (2002). *A report on the effect of the unitedstreaming™ application on educational performance.* Cometrika, Inc., Baseline Research, LLC, and Longwood University.

Burden, P. R., & Byrd, D. M. (2003). *Methods for effective teaching* (3rd ed.). Boston: Allyn & Bacon.

Cotton, K. (1992). *Computer-assisted instruction. Northwest Regional Educational Laboratory.* Retrieved March 28, 2007, from http://www.nwrel.org/scpd/sirs/5/cu10.html.

Cradler, R., & Cradler, J. (1999). *Just in time: Technology innovation challenge grant year 2 evaluation report for Blackfoot School District no. 55.* San Mateo, CA: Educational Support Systems.

Gardner, H. (1999). *Intelligence reframed: Multiple intelligences for the 21st century.* New York: Basic Books.

Hepburn, K. S. (2006). *Building culturally and linguistically competent services for young children, their families, and school readiness.* Baltimore, MD: The Anne E. Casey Foundation, Georgetown University Center for Child and Human Development. Accessed November 18, 2006, at http://www.aecf.org/upload/publicationfiles/HS3622H325.pdf.

McHale, T. (2005, September). Portrait of a digital native. *Technology & Learning,* 33–34.

Middleton, B. M., & Murray, R. K. (1999). The impact of instructional technology on student academic achievement in reading and mathematics. *International Journal of Instructional Media, 26*(1), 109.

Prensky, M. (2001). Digital natives, digital immigrants. *On the Horizon,* 9(5), 1–6.

Reutzel, D. R., & Cooter, R. B. (2000). *Teaching children to read* (3rd ed.). Upper Saddle River, NJ: Merrill/Prentice Hall.

Scardamalia, M., & Bereiter, C. (1996). Computer support for knowledge-building communities. In T. Kotchmann (Ed.), *CSCI: Theory and practice of an emerging paradigm.* Mahwah, NJ: Lawrence Erlbaum Associates.

Sivin-Kachala, J., & Bialo, E. (1994). *Report on the effectiveness of technology in schools, 1990–1994.* Washington, DC: Software Publishers Association.

Sousa, D. A. (2001). *How the brain learns: A classroom teacher's guide* (2nd ed.). Thousand Oaks, CA: Corwin Press.

Tomlinson, C. A. (2001). *How to differentiate instruction in mixed ability classrooms* (2nd ed.). Alexandria, VA: Association for Supervision and Curriculum Development.

Underwood, J., & Brown, J. (Eds.) (1997). *Integrated learning system: Potential into practice.* Oxford, UK: Heinemann/NCET.

Willis, J. W. (2006). *Research-based strategies to ignite student learning.* Alexandria, VA: Association for Supervision and Curriculum Development.

Creating a Lesson Plan

Objective: Understand the parts of a lesson plan.

1.1 Write a direct instruction lesson, defining each element.

1.2 Write an inquiry lesson plan, incorporating student choice and at least one essential question.

Continuing our road trip analogy, a lesson plan involves putting all our advance planning ideas into a real plan of action to create an itinerary (Figure 8.1, p. 116). The plan tells us where we are going, how we'll get there, what we plan to see and do, and what we need to pack. Once you begin to teach the lesson, you begin the journey!

Relevant INTASC Principles: #1, #2, #3, #4, #5, #6, #7, #8, #9 (See inside back cover of this book for complete list.)

PUTTING THE PIECES TOGETHER

> *If a task has once begun*
> *Never leave it till it's done*
> *Be the labor great or small*
> *Do it well or not at all.*
>
> —Anonymous

Teachers identify the lesson topic, find curricular standards associated with the content, write the objective, and then create the assessment. Instructional strategies and lesson materials are chosen and collected. Those steps can be considered the **preplanning stage**; the legwork, if you will, of planning a lesson. Then the actual lesson plan is written, which can be called the **formal planning stage.**

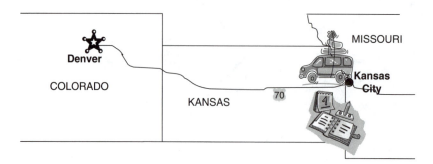

FIGURE 8.1   Creating a Road Trip Itinerary

Lesson plans are not written for teachers to read to the class. They are used to structure the lesson. A **lesson plan** is a sequence of procedural instructions that explain how the identified content will be taught, when and how to use materials, and how to assess what was learned throughout the lesson. A lesson plan puts the procedural statements of instruction in a sequential order to create a smooth flow. A well-written and organized plan allows for seamless transitions from one part to the next. The lesson plan should also be written so concepts are developed and materials used from the most concrete to the more abstract. Though there are many lesson plan formats, every lesson plan is organized to contain a *beginning, middle,* and *end.*

Before a teacher starts organizing the learning experience by formally writing the lesson plan, he must decide which type or method of learning experience he wishes to use. There are two main types of instructional delivery: direct and indirect. Typically, **direct instruction** is considered **teacher-centered instruction.** Chall (2000) found the teacher-centered approach to teaching had a more formal, traditional pattern of instruction when compared to the more indirect, **student-centered instruction.**

Meyer (1984) defines **indirect instruction** as an "approach where the process of learning is inquiry, the result is discovery, and learning context is specific to problem-solving" (p. 383). The term *indirect instruction* is commonly used to name any method in which the student is actively, rather than passively, engaged (Marchesani, 2007). Jarolimek, Foster, and Kellough (2005) refer to direct instruction as a *delivery or expository method* while indirect instruction is considered an *access method.*

In direct instruction, the teacher directly delivers instruction. In indirect lessons, students access information for themselves through various experiences planned by the teacher, with collaboration between the students and the teacher. In actual practice, teachers may combine some forms of each approach depending on their students' learning styles, the lesson's content, and teaching situations (Kellough & Roberts, 2002). Though both approaches encourage student learning of facts, knowledge, and skills, there are differences in their instructional delivery. Refer to Figure 8.2 to visualize the instructional approach continuum.

Instructional Approach Continuum		
Teacher Centered		**Student Centered**
Direct Instruction	▲	**Indirect Instruction**
Process:		**Process:**
Presentation		Inquiry
Explanation		Discovery
Reinforcement		Problem solving
Expository Method		**Access Method**

FIGURE 8.2   Instructional Approach Continuum

Section I: Direct Instruction Lessons

What Is Direct Instruction?

A direct instruction lesson is exactly what the term implies. Teachers give content information directly to the students using a variety of instructional strategies. "Direct instruction is a highly structured, teacher-centered strategy that capitalizes on such behavioral techniques as modeling, feedback, and reinforcement to promote basic skill acquisition" (Morrison, 2000, p. 523). There are several other terms for direct instruction, and a brief list includes: *teacher instruction, expository teaching, direct teaching, directive teaching,* and *teacher-centered instruction* (Jarolimek et al., 2005; Salsbury, 2002). "Teacher-centered learning fits the classic view of education, with its emphasis on student knowledge and skills" (Chall, 2000, p. 7).

Teacher-directed instruction is a highly organized instructional approach emphasizing distinct student goals, extensive content coverage with the use of related materials, and consistent monitoring of student performance within a linearly structured plan, while supplying immediate feedback to students (Ellis & Fouts, 1997; Morrison, 2000). Direct instruction is goal-oriented teaching with scaffolded procedures built in. "Teachers provide instructional scaffolding in a variety of ways, including breaking complex skills into subskills, asking facilitating questions, presenting examples, modeling the steps in solving problems, and providing prompts and cues" (Kauchak & Eggen, 2007, p. 223).

A wide range of instructional strategies are considered elements of direct instruction. Direct teaching of facts, concepts, generalizations, and skills to students by the teacher are characteristics of direct instruction and may usually be found in the form of lecture (Smith, 1997). Lecture, teacher-led discussion, drill and practice, textbooks, and teacher-led question/answer sessions are representative of the multitude of teacher-centered instructional opportunities found in the classroom (Chall, 2000; Salsbury, 2002; Smith, 1986). Experienced teachers may present age-appropriate content through lecture, yet they utilize a wide variety of materials throughout the lesson to ensure students find the information relevant.

Concepts are types of content that can be taught effectively with teacher-directed instruction. Concepts are categories of ideas that can be illustrated by examples through their characteristics and understanding of their relationships (Kellough & Roberts, 2002). The direct instruction approach focuses on teaching the essential characteristics of a concept's specific features or attributes when a teacher models representations and provides examples (Kauchak & Eggen, 2007).

The direct instruction lesson plan presented in this chapter is sequential and contains multiple elements, though the basic format only has three distinct sections: the beginning, middle, and end. The lesson plan elements are (1) motivation, (2) goal for learner statement, (3) teaching new content, (4) modeling, (5) guided practice, (6) independent practice, (7) checking for understanding, (8) application used for assessment, and (9) closure. These elements are derived from work done by Madeline Hunter and her UCLA colleagues in the 1970s. Dr. Hunter suggested various elements that might be considered when planning effective instruction. In practice, these elements were compiled by others and called the "Hunter Model" whose elements were (1) anticipatory set, (2) statement of objective, (3) teaching, (4) modeling, (5) checking for understanding, (6) guided practice, and (7) independent practice (Goldberg, 1990).

The lesson plan elements in this text parallel Hunter's early work and further define what is happening in effective lessons today. They also reflect newer research, especially in the area of brain-based learning. Closure, for example, is a separate plan element "because of the high impact this strategy has on improving retention of learning" (Sousa, 2001, p. 286). And Hunter's anticipatory set is now called motivation to emphasize the importance of relevance in helping students learn new information and skills (Sousa, 2001).

It is important to remember that all lessons may not contain all the elements, or the elements may be flexibly sequenced within the plan. Ultimately, it is up to the teacher to decide which lesson plan components are essential to include within a specific lesson plan. Refer to Figure 8.3 for the lesson planning format of a direct instruction lesson.

Writing a Direct Instruction Lesson Plan: The Elements Defined

We can have facts without thinking but we cannot have thinking without facts.

—John Dewey

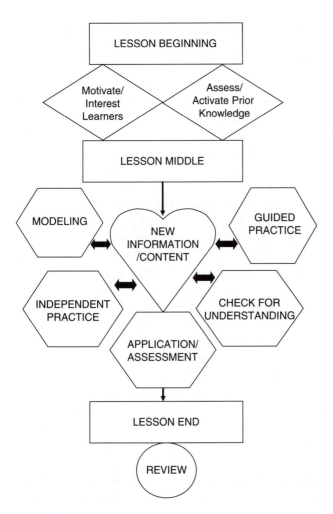

FIGURE 8.3 Direct Instruction Lesson Plan Format and Flow

Lesson Beginning During the beginning of the lesson, a teacher introduces the topic and explains the lesson's objective in "student language." In this format, this is called the *goal for learner statement.* It is important for students to know from the beginning what they will be learning and what they will be expected to do to demonstrate their understanding. Imagine, for example, that one group of students is told at the beginning of a lesson that they will be studying adjectives. Then another group of students is told they will be studying adjectives and will be using adjectives at the end of the lesson to write a paragraph describing a picture. The second group of students is, of course, more informed and able to focus more intently on *using* adjectives and not just on what they are or how they are formed.

Education is not the filling of a pail, but the lighting of a fire.
—William Butler Yeats

A teacher gains students' attention and encourages their interest in the topic by activating prior knowledge and establishing relevancy through books, materials, or a brief activity. In this book's lesson plan format, gaining attention and encouraging student interest at the beginning of the lesson is referred to as **motivation.** "Learners of all ages are more motivated when they can see the usefulness of what they are learning and when they can use that information to do something that has an impact on others—especially their local community" (National Research Council, 2000, p. 61). It may also be necessary at this time to clear up and correct any misconceptions of the topic, and to give students opportunities now to explore materials that will be used more thoroughly later in the lesson.

Give some thought about how to transition from this stage of the lesson into the middle of the lesson. There should be an easy flow from one to the other without an abrupt disruption to the teaching. The transition may be procedural. If the students have been gathered together near the teacher listening to a story or handling realia, the teacher may then ask students to return the items to her desk, return to their desks, and retrieve their pencils. Or the transition may be related to the lesson's content. The teacher may say, "That video clip showed Spanish-speaking people shopping. Write down the Spanish words of three items you remember hearing in the video."

Lesson Middle The middle of the lesson contains several opportunities for a teacher to deliver content information to students through a variety of instructional strategies and the use of a variety of materials, and for students to interact with the content through activities and materials. Teachers may deliver the **content information,** concepts, processes, and generalizations entirely through lecture. They may provide structures to help students learn content. Teachers may, however, decide to include indirect, student-centered activities to ensure students are actively involved in the learning process. Marzano, Pickering, and Pollock (2001) suggest using advance graphic organizers, questions, and cues as tools to help students organize information. "Since there are limits on the amount of information that people can hold in short-term memory, short-term memory is enhanced when people are able to chunk information into familiar patterns" (Bransford, Brown, & Cocking, 2000, p. 33).

Whether or not the lesson contains a lot of new information or review information, it is a good idea to break up the content into smaller, more manageable chunks with opportunities for the students to *practice* using the content. "It is not until students have practiced upwards of about 24 times that they reach 80% competency" (Marzano et al., 2001, p. 67). However, after only four practice sessions, students can reach a competency level of approximately 48%. This is important to keep in mind when developing a lesson plan. Building in *guided and independent practice opportunities* becomes extremely important to ensure learning occurs.

Guided practice refers to students practicing new skills and knowledge with others, including other students, and with guidance from the teacher. Depending on the type of practice activity, teachers may structure practice sessions with the entire group of students or within small groups. Guided practice may be organized to increase student participation and social interaction (National Research Council, 2000; Starko et al., 2003). Teachers want students to gain confidence in their newly acquired knowledge during practice activities and find peer interaction beneficial at this time, so they will monitor students as they work together and provide immediate feedback on their practice.

Off and on throughout the middle of the lesson, teachers **model** how to complete various activities and use lesson materials, as well as model how to think about the content (Burden & Byrd, 2003; Starko et al., 2003). Students need to experience how skilled learners, like the teacher, think through processes. They can do so with appropriate modeling and facilitation from their teachers. When teachers, for example, end an activity with reflective questions, students become conscious of their own cognitive processes and learn to monitor their work and thinking; in other words, they learn how to learn.

Independent practice refers to learners practicing the information alone. "Practice is intended to consolidate, clarify, and emphasize what the student has already learned (Burden & Byrd, 2003). There are many instructional strategies, such as centers, learning contracts, and others (Tomlinson, 1999–2000), that support practice. Teachers must decide when they think individual students are ready to try their new skills alone and which students still need the safety net of continued guided practice.

> *That which we persist in doing becomes easier, not that the task itself has become easier, but that our ability to perform it has improved.*
>
> —Ralph Waldo Emerson

Asking questions throughout the lesson is critical to ensure students are learning and understanding the content. Research (Cotton, 2006) indicates that questioning is second only to lecturing in popularity as a teaching method, and that classroom teachers spend anywhere from 35% to 50% of their instructional time asking questions. Questioning motivates students to become involved in their learning experiences (Eggen & Kauchak, 2006; National Research Council, 2000). Reasons to ask questions include: (1) to check for understanding; (2) to focus and redirect student attention on the task or process; (3) to have students repeat directional procedures (e.g., which materials to collect for the activity); (4) to stimulate higher level thinking; and (5) to elaborate on their work. On average, approximately 60% of the questions asked during instruction are lower cognitive questions, 20% are higher cognitive questions, and 20% are procedural (Cotton, 2006).

To *check for understanding,* teachers ask a series of content-related questions during instruction. Lower level questions could be answered by all students at the same time. For example, students could write brief answers to questions on an individual chalkboard, or they could use hand signals to signal yes or no answers. The length of time teachers wait for a response after posing a question is called **wait time.** The average wait time teachers allow after posing a question is 1 second or less. Increasing wait time beyond 3 seconds is positively related to improved student achievement (Cotton, 2006; Sousa, 2001), and that is an important fact to keep in mind during the middle part of your lesson.

Another component of the middle of the lesson is to give students the opportunity to apply what they have learned. This *application* of the content can provide documentation of whether the students have achieved the knowledge required to reach the lesson objective. Individual students apply what they have learned from the entire lesson by completing an **assessment assignment.** These application assignments may be informal or formal assessments, ungraded or graded. They may take the form of the creation of some product such as a poem or mural. They may also be formative, such as a set of math problems to provide evidence of progress, or summative, such as a quiz to evaluate students' learning at the end of instruction. Refer back to chapter 5 for a more complete list and explanation of assessments.

Lesson End   The end of the lesson provides **closure.** This stage could include a brief, yet active review of the concepts and skills

Reality Check

Question: How do you check students' understanding?

My favorite way to check the understanding of students in math is using dry erase slates. I'll give them a problem (usually on the overhead or orally) and every student has to write the answer on his or her slate. When they hold up an answer, it is an instant way for me to see whether or not they have mastered the concept. Plus, I can see if several students are making the same mistake and help them to retrace their steps. By using slates, I can avoid repeating a lesson or concept to kids that already know how to do it.

Usually, I'll do a quick check of a skill and write down the names of students who need more practice. Then when they have work time, I'll pull those kids in a small group to review the area they're struggling with. Actually, the best things about this method are that it requires *zero* grading on my part and that it requires every student to answer a question (not just the ones that volunteer all the time).

Carrie Smith
Prairie Vista Elementary School
Fourth- and fifth-grade multiage

taught throughout the lesson. Teachers may want to guide the closure procedures by asking key questions and allowing students' oral, written, or even physical responses. This is also one more chance for teachers to clear up any content-related misconceptions. Materials used earlier in the lesson can be revisited to clarify the content review.

Closure is also a good time for students to share what they learned, either oral summaries of ideas or through the presentation of the product they created for their assessment assignment. Closure gives teachers the opportunity again to discuss reasons for learning the content, how the information is connected to the "real" world, and even prepare students for tomorrow's learning sessions (Kauchak & Eggen, 2007). Some teachers find it necessary, due to time constraints, type of instruction, or other reasons, to conduct the closure *before* giving students the opportunity to apply what they learned by completing an assessment assignment.

The following lesson plan examples demonstrate the flow and structure of direct instruction for elementary and high school students. The same format applies to middle school lesson plans. As you read through the lesson plans, compare not only the basic organization to other lesson plan formats you may be familiar with or find online, but the teachers' writing styles, activity choices, instructional strategies, groupings, and other elements affected by teacher planning decisions.

PULLING IT ALL TOGETHER: EXAMPLE A
DIRECT INSTRUCTION LESSON PLAN

Topic: Classification of Animals

Grade Level: 4th

Subject Area: Science

Standard: 1. Living things can be classified by characteristics.

Objective: Classify animals.

    1.1. Identify animals as carnivore, herbivore, or omnivore.

Materials:

Books: *The Skull Alphabet Book* or *The Extinct Alphabet Book,* by Jerry Pallotta (1993, 2002) with illustrations by Ralph Masiello; *Iktomi and the Buffalo Skull* by Paul Goble (1991)

Real animal skulls	Visuals/posters/photographs of skulls
Overhead projector	Overhead transparency of chart
Measuring tapes	Rulers
Computer/projector	Paper and pencils
World map	Desktop maps (optional)

Web sites: Animal Planet (2006), http://animal.discovery.com/guides/atoz/atoz.html; World Almanac for Kids (2006), http://www.worldalmanacforkids.com/html

Lesson Beginning

- Introduce and read aloud one of the books. While reading, show images and ask questions to activate students' prior knowledge of animal characteristics and needs for survival. Have students informally compare how the characteristics of animal heads are different, especially when they look at the various types of teeth.
- Give the main goal of the lesson to the students. Explain to them that they will examine and compare animal skulls to determine which is a carnivore, herbivore, or omnivore.

Lesson Middle

- Review information (from previous lessons) on survival needs, such as water, shelter, and food.
- Describe and explain similar and different characteristics of carnivores, herbivores, and omnivores, such as the types of food they would eat, their habitats, and survival needs.
- Point out animal habitats' locations on a map.
- Lead a discussion on the various types of vegetation available at the different locations for food and habitats/shelter using visual images from Web sites, photographs, and posters. Explain that animal teeth are adapted to match the various types of foods they eat in their habitats. For

example, herbivores eat plants most of the time, and their teeth are similar to human molars so they can grind up plants (leaves, twigs, etc.). A carnivore eats other animals most of the time, so it has teeth that were adapted to tear and rip up meat as well as crack bones. An animal that eats both plants and animals is called an omnivore; its teeth will have adapted similar characteristics of both types of teeth. It is important to remember that the matching of tooth form to its function is one way animals have evolved and adapted to fit their environment.

- Throughout the lesson, ask various types of questions to check for understanding (e.g., What do longer canine teeth tell you about the animal?), focus attention (e.g., Where on the map would you expect a beaver to live? Point to it on your desk map.), and have students repeat directions (e.g., What are you expected to locate on the map?). Ask additional questions as needed.

- Model how to categorize the animal skull characteristics using a chart on the overhead projector. The chart contains room for column categories of "Animals" and row categories of "Characteristics," such as "Teeth."

- Display three types of skulls. For this example, focus on the "Teeth" characteristic (shape, length, color, etc.).

- Point out the facial feature in each skull such as the teeth.

- Use a measuring tape to gauge the length of the canine teeth in the three skulls. Record the information on the chart under "Teeth."

- Explain the process of gathering data from the three skulls, remembering to orally explain any decisions and rationales for the decisions.

- Model thinking process for adding a skull characteristic to the chart; in this case, add "Number of Teeth." Model the process of counting teeth and recording the data. Ask students to think of other categories that could be added to the chart based on their observation of skulls' characteristics. If necessary, use questions to lead students to add such categories as "Food," "Location."

- Model how to add characteristics to the chart, then assign the animal to the category of omnivore, herbivore, or carnivore. Ask students questions about the animal characteristics of each category: Why do you think that animal is an omnivore? If the animal has long, red front teeth, what type of food would it eat?

- Then split students up into 6 groups of 4 students each.

- Have students create their own charts, patterning theirs after the example displayed on the overhead, though they may include additional categories.

- Hand out a skull to each group.

- Guide students through the process of measuring one skull feature and recording the data.

- Give students the opportunity to practice collecting and recording data in their groups using the skulls. Have students measure various features, such as teeth, eye sockets, and skull diameters, to determine similarities and differences between the animals.

- Continue a rotation process between groups at least twice to give students practice gathering, recording, and analyzing data from assorted skulls.

- Check that all groups have recorded the data and assigned skulls to categories of omnivore, herbivore, or carnivore.

- Assign students to individually apply what they learned from their investigations by categorizing two skulls they had not examined during the lesson.
- Have students sketch the skull on a piece of paper, then label data of each skull on the sketch, using their earlier chart as a reference.
- Give students criteria for the assessment assignment: (1) gather data from skulls, (2) record data on sketch, (3) analyze data, and (4) categorize and label animals.

Lesson End

- Gather students together on the floor to share an interesting discovery from their investigation.
- Ask questions occasionally to encourage students to keep on review topics.
- Explain the importance of identifying the different types of animals, their habitats, and relationships to the students' real world.
- Collect assignments for evaluation using criteria.

PULLING IT ALL TOGETHER: EXAMPLE B
DIRECT INSTRUCTION LESSON PLAN

Topic: Foreign Countries

Grade Level/Subject: High School Foreign Language

Standard: 3. Connect with other disciplines.

   3.1 Students reinforce and further their knowledge of other disciplines through the foreign language.

Objective: Locate and name foreign countries in the news.

   1.1 Label foreign countries in the foreign language on a world map.
   1.2 Orally name and point out one foreign country using the foreign language.

Materials: large world map with country outlines and names in English (floor or wall); country labels in the foreign language; individual student world map outlines; world map outline for the overhead projector (identical to the student map; video clip of traveling family; flags; recording of national anthem

Lesson Beginning

As the students enter the classroom, have flags of various countries hanging in the classroom; have the national anthem of the target language playing; have posters and magazines of various countries displayed on a bulletin board, classroom wall, or chalkboard; and hand each student a "passport" and an outline map of the world.

Once students are seated, show a video clip of a family traveling around the world, going through customs in various countries, and having their passports stamped. The video clip also shows a world map with each "new" country highlighted and labeled in the foreign language being studied in class. In the target language, explain what the students just saw, pointing to and naming each country visited in the video on the large world map. Point out the displays in the room, read aloud some of the headlines of countries in the news, and tell the students that they will be learning the names of various foreign countries in the news in the target language and locating the countries on a world map.

Lesson Middle

Move to the overhead, point to a country, and say its name in the target language. Ask the class to repeat the name several times, repeating after you. Then ask students to turn to a neighbor and say, "That is _____ " and reply, "Yes, that is _____ ." Countries are only labeled in English at this point, but students are hearing and responding with the country's name in the target language.

Next, label the country's name in the target language on the overhead map. Direct the students to label the country and repeat the name aloud. Move around the room to check for accuracy and engage individuals in conversation about the map or the country's name or location.

Continue following this pattern for the rest of the countries. After all the countries are labeled, check students' recall and understanding by erasing one country label at a time from the overhead map. At this point, students can still look at their own individual maps for help.

Put students into small groups and direct them to use the phrases, "Where is _____ ," "_____ is (direction; such as north of) _____ ," "_____ is on the continent of _____ ," and "_____ is in the news." Walk around the room to monitor pronunciation.

Display the large world wall or floor map and the labels for the countries studied. Then direct various students to place the labels on the appropriate country, saying its name as the label is placed. Use total physical response (TPR) commands to reinforce the learning process and to include all students. For example, "Come to the large map and show me Spain. Touch England. Point to Saudi Arabia. Find China. On your map, color Israel green."

Collect practice maps. Hand out world maps copied on $8\frac{1}{2} \times 11$ sheets of paper with blank lines within the boundaries of each county studied. List the countries' names on the board or overhead and instruct each student to label the countries in the target language. Walk around and ask each child one question that will require the student to use the name and point to one of the countries studied.

Lesson End

Have each student open his or her passport and create a simple colored geometric shaped "stamp" for each country studied today, labeling each in the target language and English. Put the students into small groups to display and explain in the target language what they wrote and drew. For example, "I drew a red circle and wrote Japan in French and English." Monitor students and use a checklist to note which students responded correctly and which need help with pronunciation, word choice, or grammar.

YOUR TURN

 ACTIVITY 1: Evaluation of a Direct Instruction Lesson Plan

INTASC Principles 7, 9, and 10

Directions: Form a small group. Refer to either of the sample lesson plans written in "Pulling It Together: Lesson Plan Example A or B." As a group, answer the following questions.

1. Critique the lesson materials.

   a. Did the teacher use 1 piece of literature (print material), 2 activities, and 2 visual aids? If not, what was omitted?

   b. What could the teacher add to improve the overall quality of the lesson?

2. Identify the elements of a direct instruction plan within the sample lesson plan. You may want to highlight or underline key statements. Put a check mark in front of each of the following elements as you find them.

_____	Motivation	_____	Goal for learner statement
_____	Modeling	_____	Presenting content information
_____	Guided practice	_____	Checking for understanding
_____	Independent practice	_____	Closure
_____	Application assignment/assessment		

3. Were any direct instruction lesson plan elements missing? If so, which ones? Why do you think the teacher omitted it/them?

4. Were any elements used more than once? If so, which ones? Why do you think it/they were used more than once?

 ACTIVITY 2: Write a Basic 3-Part Direct Instruction Lesson Plan

INTASC Principles 1, 4, 5, and 7

Directions: Write a lesson using the format of the sample(s) above, or merely identify what you will do for each element by writing terms or phrases. If you omit any of the elements, write a brief explanation why.

Use the information you gathered during the preplanning stage to help guide your lesson plan development.

1. Identify the following lesson plan elements.

   Topic:

   Grade Level or Subject:

   Standard:

TECHNOLOGY IN EDUCATION

If you wish, go to http://www.lessonplans.com/ and use the **lesson plan generator**.

To see **complete lesson plans** that you can adapt or use to stimulate your thinking, go to Thinkfinity at http://www.marcopolo-education.org/home.aspx. This site's content partners are the national subject area organizations.

Objective:

Materials:

Beginning:

Middle:

End:

Suggesion: You may use the lesson planner identified in the TiE box to generate your plan. You may also find it helpful to look at other complete lesson plans.

 ACTIVITY 3: Reflection

INTASC Principle 9

Directions: Answer the following question.

1. Compare the lesson plan you wrote in Activity 2 to your "remembered" lesson plan in chapter 1. How are they the same? How are they different?

Section II: Indirect Instruction

Every truth has four corners: as a teacher I give you one corner, and it is for you to find the other three.

—Confucius

What Is Indirect Instruction?

Indirect instruction refers to the style of information delivery. Whereas direct instruction is a delivery or expository method, indirect instruction is considered an **access method** (Jarolimek et al., 2005). In *direct* instruction, the teacher directly delivers instruction. *Indirect* instruction is at the opposite end of the instructional continuum and gives students opportunities to access information for themselves through various experiences planned by the teacher, in collaboration between the students and the teacher, or by the students themselves (Marzano, Norford, Paynter, Pickering, & Gaddy, 2001; Pasch, Langer, Gardner, Starko, & Moody, 1995). Access mode lessons can also be called *inquiry, problem-solving,* or *guided discovery learning.* The indirect lesson format in this book will follow guidelines for creating an inquiry lesson.

Inquiry is a type of problem solving; answering questions and solving problems based on the examination of facts and through observations (Joyce, Weil, & Calhoun, 2000). Inquiry has always been a part of education. Socrates taught his students through aggressive questioning, leading his students to discover learning for themselves. In the early 20th century, John Dewey developed and introduced the first inquiry-based learning methods in the United States. Dewey advocated a child-centered approach to learning based on providing real-world experiences (Center for Learning and Technology, 1999).

It is a huge mistake to assume that this type of learning means turning students loose to discover things on their own. "This perspective confuses a theory of pedagogy [teaching] with a theory of knowing" (National Research Council, 2000, p. 11). If teachers monitor students' interests, changing perspectives, and knowledge, then they can adapt their lesson planning to accommodate active learners. Teachers must still plan carefully in order to provide instructional scaffolding (DiVesta, 1987).

Planning and Implementing Indirect Inquiry Learning

Inquiry-based learning is not unstructured—just differently structured. The plan will still have a beginning, middle, and end. The teacher still has to know the content, and "storeroom knowledge" is perhaps even more important. The planning process for direct instruction and indirect (inquiry) lessons is nearly identical.

Reality Check

Question: Do you use indirect instruction? If so, how do the students respond?

A lesson on assembly lines and production during the Industrial Revolution:

Shannon: Hey look, Mrs. Sutton has all kinds of stuff on the desks today. I wonder what we are doing?

Ali: It looks like we are building something. At least we won't have to read from the book today.

Donnie: I love it when Mrs. Sutton does this stuff. I wonder what we are going to do with the packing peanuts and the toothpicks.

Shannon: There is also a picture of something on the desks. It is called a widget, and it is made out of these things.

Donnie: We have been studying factories and the industrial revolution. Maybe it has something to do with that.

Mrs. Sutton: OK, guys, take your seats. Today we are going to form groups. One group will be tradesmen who specialize in making widgets, a fictional product. These people will build the product from start to finish alone. The other group will be part of an assembly line where each person is in charge of only one part of the assembly.

After the lesson . . .

Donnie: Man, that was cool. Who knew that assembly line would be so much faster? You know?

Shannon: Yeah, the assembly line was faster, but I think the tradesmen did better work. I think you do better work when you are alone because you can't blame mistakes on someone else.

Ali: Yeah, I think you are right. I guess people just wanted more stuff and they wanted it cheaper. They had to give up on some of the quality in order to increase the quantity. That's what Mrs. Sutton was talking about yesterday. I guess I didn't understand it until I saw it in action.

Michelle Sutton
Shelbyville Middle School

Inquiry lesson planning starts with the selection of a topic, academic standards, and writing an objective. Good and Brophy (2000) state, "(l)earning can be couched within an applications context and students can be engaged in higher-order thinking about a topic right from the beginning of [inquiry] instruction" (p. 417). Teachers must also plan how to select materials and resources, and determine the method of inquiry and product options. Inquiry can range from being highly structured by the teacher (see Lesson Plan Sample C at the end of this chapter) to giving students more control of the inquiry process (see Lesson Plan Sample D at the end of this chapter). Teachers must carefully consider the students and their familiarity with more independent learning situations when deciding how much structure is needed during the inquiry phase.

Inquiry lessons still begin by motivating the learners and setting goals. In the middle part of an indirect lesson, students are actively investigating a topic. By the end of the lesson, students are demonstrating what they learned. Refer to Figure 8.4 for the lesson plan format of an indirect lesson plan, then compare it to the format of Figure 8.3.

The planning stage may be nearly the same for direct instruction and inquiry lessons, yet the implementation is quite different. The role of the teacher in inquiry learning is that of a facilitator, rather than a dispenser of knowledge. A common phrase to describe the different role is that a teacher is the "guide on the side" rather than a "sage on a stage." Teachers who elect to use an inquiry-based learning approach

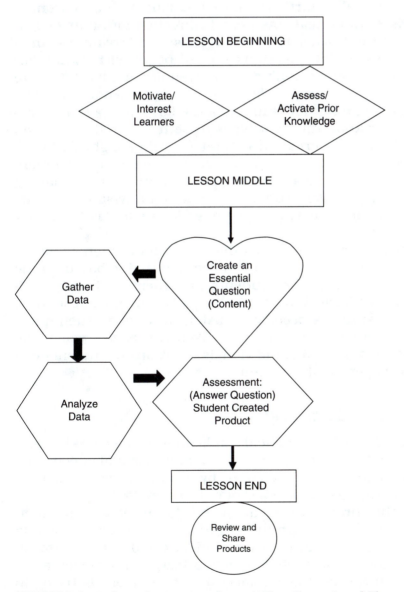

FIGURE 8.4 Indirect Instruction Lesson Plan Format and Flow

help students identify and refine their questions and guide the research, inquiry, and reporting processes.

Wisdom begins in wonder.

—Socrates

Writing Essential Questions

Inquiry learning centers around constructing knowledge and understanding through answering questions. Students should not be searching for answers about minutiae. Instead, well-designed inquiry learning should lead to conceptual understanding. Inquiry in education should be about helping students form a greater understanding of the world in which they live.

Students usually start their investigations with an essential question. **Essential questions** provide direction for an investigation and lead the learner to *make a decision* or *create a plan of action*. Most essential questions do *not* begin with "what is." "What is" type questions don't generally require an investigator to make a decision or create a plan. For example, "What is a habitat?" will lead to finding a definition of the term and perhaps help the investigator know different types. A better essential question might be, "How can I create a habitat for wild songbirds in my neighborhood?" This will help the student create a plan of action. "Should our school have a recycling plan?" would lead to making a decision. For younger students, it is often advisable to start them with "I wonder how . . ." type questions such as "I wonder how plants grow?"

Whether the teacher provides the essential question or allows the students to create their own is a decision that is based on the teacher's knowledge of the students and their familiarity with inquiry. It is most likely that the teacher will create the question, at least until the students become accustomed to using such questions to guide investigation. And most likely the teacher will create many questions from which individuals or groups of students can select the most personally relevant.

Assessment of Learning

Inquiry learning is the practical application of basic skills and knowledge. Students investigate to answer an essential question by providing a solution to a problem or by creating a plan of action. The students will need to demonstrate their results.

They do this through the creation and sharing of some product. If a student decided through investigation that the school should have a recycling program, then the student could write a letter to the school principal or possibly create a PowerPoint presentation to be shown at a school board meeting. The student is trying to inform and persuade through the completed product. If a student

```
┌─────────────────────────────────────────────────────────────┐
│                   Sample Product Ideas                       │
│                                                              │
│ Written Products                                             │
│                                                              │
│ Essay              Editorial              News Article       │
│                                                              │
│ Poem               Song Lyrics            Letter             │
│                    ───────────                               │
│ Oral Products                                                │
│                                                              │
│ Debate             A Speech               A Play             │
│                                                              │
│ Commercial         News Broadcast         Song              │
│                    ─────────────                             │
│ Media Products                                               │
│                                                              │
│ PowerPoint         Photo Essay            Mural              │
│                                                              │
│ Diagram            3-D Model              Collage            │
│                                                              │
└─────────────────────────────────────────────────────────────┘
```

FIGURE 8.5   Sample Product Ideas

group decided through an investigation that the school could attract birds by providing birdhouses and bird feeders, they could build them and place them in an appropriate location outside the school building.

The products should be logical methods of explaining what was learned through the investigation. It is often helpful to tell the students to select an audience for their product. Who would need or want to know the information? How best could you tell that audience what you found out? Refer to Figure 8.5 for sample product ideas.

A sense of curiosity is nature's original school of education.
—Smiley Blanton

IN SUMMARY

Direct instruction is sometimes the better choice, especially when time is an issue. Direct instruction is the most efficient method of disseminating basic information: reading and math skills, for example. Teachers, though, also want students to inquire on their own, to use problem-solving strategies when they're confronted with problems. Inquiry lessons allow students to apply the knowledge and skills they learned through experiencing direct instruction.

If students have learned how to figure area in mathematics, they could complete an inquiry that would apply that knowledge. Their investigation could answer the essential question, "What would be the best carpet to use in our new media center?" Students would have to determine the amount of carpet needed by using their knowledge of how to figure area. Then they would have to examine the price of various carpets and determine what types would stand up best under heavy usage. This investigation would be the practical application of their basic skills to solve a real-life problem.

An effective teacher uses both direct and indirect instructional methods. Selecting which strategy is better than the other is one more decision-making opportunity for the professional educator.

 UNIT CONNECTION

A unit of instruction will most likely contain both direct instruction and inquiry learning opportunities. Often a teacher will use direct instruction to provide students with basic knowledge and skills that will be used in the inquiry process.

PULLING IT ALL TOGETHER: EXAMPLE C
INDIRECT INSTRUCTION LESSON PLAN

This inquiry lesson plan is more teacher-centered than student-centered. The teacher has created the investigations and provided the reference materials.

Topic: Conservation

Grade Level: 3rd grade

Lesson Objective:

1. Collect and organize data, and report findings.
    1.1 Create a plan of action for creating a wildlife habitat.

Relevant Academic Standards:

Science 3.1.2 Participate in different types of guided investigations and observations.

Science 3.1.3 Keep and report records of investigations and observations.

Essential Question: How can I plan a habitat for a bird?

(Problem solving)

Materials:

—field journals for each child
—bird identification book
—information packets for each child that contain black outlines of birds with short descriptions of their habitats

Before the lesson begins: Display pictures of native or migratory birds for your area. Label each picture with the bird's common name.

Beginning

Motivation: Ask, "What do we know about birds?" "What do they need to survive?" Record answers on a class chart. Then tell the students that we will be observing birds outside and learning about what they need to survive so that we can plan habitats for them.

Middle

Procedure:

1. Define habitat for the students. Show pictures of various habitats that provide shelter and food for birds in the area (e.g., a wetland, a field, a forest, or all of these).
2. Hand out the outlines of the birds. Allow time for the students to find the birds around the room and to color their birds to match. Explain that this will help them know what birds they will be seeing when they go outside. Have them read the short descriptions of the birds' habitats.
3. Once at the observation site, the students select one bird to watch for 10 minutes. They should complete their field study notes.

Students will be asked to identify the weather, time of day, date, the location of observation, describe the habitat, identify the bird they observed, and note its behavior. Did it stay in trees? Did it stay on the ground, in and around bushes? Was it near water?

4. Upon returning from the observation, allow students to share what they observed.

Ask students to describe the bird they watched and to point to its picture on the wall or bulletin board.

5. Have the students refer to their field study guide to determine the habitat for their observed bird.

6. Review what was learned about habitats and from the observation.

7. Put the students in groups based on the birds they observed. It may be necessary to have more than one group for the same bird.

8. Let each group decide how they will answer the question, "How will I plan a habitat for _____ (name of bird observed)?" Provide them with a list of options that include: a drawing or diagram, a written description, a 3-D model. Provide the necessary materials.

9. Allow time for the students to complete their product.

End

10. Let each group share their product with the whole class.

Assessment

Informal: While the students share, note if they are able to identify a bird that they observed and tell one thing they observed about its habitat.

Formal: Evaluate whether each group was able to create a habitat that matched the needs of their selected bird (forest, field, water).

PULLING IT ALL TOGETHER: EXAMPLE D
INDIRECT INSTRUCTION LESSON PLAN

This lesson plan is more student-centered. The students are allowed to collaborate with the teacher to form their own essential question.

Topic: Technology and Scientific Discovery

Grade Level: 8th grade and up

Lesson Objective:

1. Understand that technology changes the lives of people and the physical environment.

    1.1 Create a product that demonstrates the impact of a selected piece of technology or scientific discovery.

Academic Standard:

Social Studies 8a: Identify and describe examples in which technology and science have changed people's lives.

Social Studies 8b: Identify and describe examples in which technology and science have led to changes in the physical environment.

Essential Question: Allow students to create their own essential questions. They should be approved by you and must have something to do with changes brought about by technology or science.

Materials:

—various reference sources including the Internet
—visuals of messenger from Ancient Greece, the Morse Code, a telegraph machine
—photos of an intact and destroyed levee
—realia including a stamped envelope
—a rotary dial phone
—a cell phone
—an e-mail message

Beginning

Motivation: Show pictures of a messenger running to deliver a message in ancient times, a telegraph machine, and Morse code, and display the realia—a rotary dial telephone, a cell phone, e-mail and text messages. Explain that the pictures and realia all show how people might communicate at various times throughout history. Discuss how the improvements can be good (more immediate) and bad (poor spelling in e-mail and text messages). Discuss the impact of the development of communication technology on human lives.

Then show a picture of a levee intact and destroyed. Ask how the levee changed the environment and the effects of its construction (provided land for homes, held back flood waters) and when it broke (destruction of homes, human and animal life, and vegetation). Discuss if building levees is a good or bad thing.

Middle

Procedure

1. Tell the students that they will be investigating changes brought about by science and technology. They can choose any technology or scientific discovery they wish and whether or not to concentrate on its impact on the environment or humans or both.

2. Explain that they will need to create an essential question to guide their investigation and that they must decide if they want to create a plan or make a decision. Write those two items on the board.

3. As a class, create lists of possible essential questions for each category.

Create a Plan	*Make a Decision*
—How can I build a better cell phone?	—Should cell phones be allowed in school?
—How can scientists use information in genetics?	—Are advances in genetic engineering good?

4. Create a class list of possible technology or scientific discoveries that could be investigated.

5. Create a class list of possible products from which students can select to demonstrate their learning.

6. Meet with each student to approve their essential question. Provide each with a list of possible questions that might further their investigation as well as a copy of the rubric that will be used to score their final product.

7. Allow investigation time. As students investigate, pose questions that will help further their search. Point them in the direction of other possible reference sources. Encourage them to interview relevant people if appropriate.

End

8. After the investigations are complete, allow each student or group of students to present their products.

9. Discuss how the investigations demonstrated how technology and science affect human lives and the environment.

Assessment

Use the following rubric to evaluate end products.

Exemplary

Individual topic selected was related to the lesson objective and represents a major or significant advance in science or technology.

Essential question is related to lesson objective and leads to the creation of a plan of action or to making a decision of importance.

Content presented is accurate, sufficient, and relevant to topic and the student.

Product is an effective method of disseminating the information.

Product is of exemplary quality.

Conclusions drawn show a depth of understanding.

Satisfactory

Individual topic selected was related to the lesson objective.

Essential question is related to the lesson objective and leads to the creation of a plan or allows for making a decision.

Content presented is accurate, sufficient, and relevant to topic.

Product is a good method for disseminating the information.

Product is complete, neat, and attractive.

Conclusions drawn are reasonable.

Unsatisfactory

Topic selected is somewhat related to the lesson objective.

Essential question is somewhat related to the lesson objective.

Student did not fully answer the essential question.

Product is incomplete.

Conclusions are not reasonable or are missing.

YOUR TURN

 ACTIVITY 1: Collaboration

INTASC Principles 1, 5, 6, 7, 9, & 10

Collaboration is an important skill for any teacher to learn and use. The old adage that two heads are better than one is true in the teaching profession. Because teachers have had different experiences, they have different perspectives to share during any collaborative session.

Directions: Get together with two or three other people who are reading this book. Make some decisions together about the following information topics and standards under Part B.

Part A

1. Select one of the following topics. Then select one of the given academic standards.

    Topic _____

    Standard _____

2. Create an essential question that would guide students during an inquiry lesson. Remember that the academic standard is broad. Your essential question may help students explore only part of the standard.

   Essential Question: _____

3. How does answering the essential question require a student to make a decision or create a plan of action?

Part B

1. Use the same topic you selected in Part A. Now select a different academic standard from the list.

   Topic _____   Standard _____

2. Create an essential question that would guide students during an inquiry lesson. Remember that the academic standard is broad. Your essential question may help students explore only part of the standard.

   Essential Question: _____

3. How does answering the essential question require a student to make a decision or create a plan of action?

Topics		
Mammals	**Inventions/Inventors**	**Culture**

Academic Standards

1. Identify and describe examples in which science and technology have changed the lives of people.
2. Describe ways in which language, stories, folktales, music, food, and artistic creations serve as expressions of culture.
3. Describe how living things adapt to their environment.
4. Measure and mix dry and liquid ingredients.
5. Make sketches and write descriptions to aid in explaining procedures or ideas.
6. Demonstrate that a great variety of living things can be sorted into groups in many ways using various features, such as how they look, where they live, and how they act, to decide which things belong to which group.
7. Make descriptive presentations that use concrete sensory details to set forth and support unified impressions of people, places, things, or experiences.

Part C—Reflection

Directions:

1. Discuss how the selection of academic standards affects the direction a lesson can take.

2. Explain how you could incorporate more than one academic standard in a single lesson. Use ideas from Parts A and B in your discussion.

ACTIVITY 2: Creating an Inquiry Lesson Plan

INTASC Principles 1, 4, 5, and 7

Directions: Use the topic and standards from your direct instruction lesson to write a lesson plan.

1. Using the topic and standard(s) you selected for your direct instruction lesson plan, create an objective. You might use the one you wrote for your lesson. You should make it as broad as possible to allow students to personalize the objective. The objective should help you create an essential question.

2. Create an essential question for the lesson. Remember to create a question that will require the students either to make a decision or create a plan of action. Remember, too, that the question should not require the students to discover minutiae or trivial information. You are trying to help them develop conceptual understanding and to apply learning in a problem-solving situation that is either a real problem or a simulation of a real problem.

   Essential Question: _____

3. List the materials your students will need in order to gather information to provide one or more possible answers to the question.

4. Write a few sentences to explain how you will introduce the essential question and motivate student interest in the experience.

5. Write a short outline of the procedure you will follow during the data gathering, organization, and interpretation process.

6. Describe how you will bring closure to the end of the lesson.

7. How will students demonstrate their learning? Write a brief explanation of the products that the students will create and how they will share their learning with you and or the class. Ideally, you will offer more than one product option, taking into consideration the various interests of your students. In this way you are differentiating the lesson product based on student interest.

8. Create a rubric that will be used to evaluate the student-generated products. Refer back to chapter 5.

ACTIVITY 3: Peer Review

INTASC Principles 9 and 10

Directions:

1. Exchange inquiry lesson plans with someone else. Look at the eight-step process you followed, then determine if your peer has followed the steps.

2. Examine their lesson's essential question. Provide written comments. Do not merely provide "rah-rah" comments like "good job" or "well done." Instead, provide corrective feedback. Tell the person what is good and also what you think could be better.

3. As you read the lesson plan, ask yourself if you would enjoy the task.

4. Complete the following checklist. Return your evaluation and orally explain it to your partner.

PEER REVIEW CHECKLIST

Peer Review for _____ (name)

Completed by _____ (your name)

_____ 1. The lesson plan has a well-worded objective that is broad enough to allow students to personalize it.

_____ 2. The academic standards match the objective.

_____ 3. The essential question will lead to solving a problem or making a decision. (Circle which one.)
Identify the problem or the decision.
_____

_____ 4. This investigation is worth the students' time; it will lead to important learning.

_____ 5. The materials are well selected.
Explain why:
_____

_____ 6. The motivation is interesting and clearly introduces the essential question.
Write the essential question:
_____

_____ 7. The procedure section explains the inquiry process in enough detail that students would be able to begin their investigation with little or no clarification needed.

_____ 8. There is more than one product option.

_____ 9. There is a rubric to evaluate the student-generated products.

Comments: _____

Activity 4: Reflection

INTASC Principle 9

Directions: Write a brief response to the following questions.

1. What decisions did you have to make to create your inquiry lesson?

2. Explain whether or not you now have a clearer understanding of the content of your lesson.

3. Did the planning process change your view of the teaching profession? Why or why not?

REFERENCES

Animal Planet. (2006). "Animals A to Zoo." Retrieved December, 2006, from http://animal.discovery.com/guides/atoz/atoz.html.

Bransford, J. D., Brown, A. L., & Cocking, R. R. (Eds.). (2000). *How people learn: Brain, mind, experience, and school.* Washington, D.C.: National Academy Press.

Burden, P. R., & Byrd, D. M. (2003). *Methods for effective teaching* (3rd ed.). Boston: Allyn & Bacon.

Center for Learning and Technology. (1999). *Inquiry learning forum.* Retrieved June 10, 2006, from http://ilf.crlt.indiana.edu/.

Chall, J. S. (2000). *The academic achievement challenge: What really works in the classroom?* New York: Guilford Press.

Cotton, K. (2006). *Classroom questioning.* North West Regional Educational Laboratory (NWREL) School Improvement Series. Retrieved March 14, 2007, from http://www.nwrel.org.

DiVesta, F. (1987). The cognitive movement and education. In J. Glover & R. Ronning (Eds.), *Historical foundations of educational psychology* (pp. 203–230). New York: Plenum.

Eggen, P. D., & Kauchak, D. P. (2006). *Strategies and models for teachers: Teaching content and thinking skills* (5th ed.). Boston: Allyn & Bacon.

Ellis, A. K., & Fouts, J. T. (1997). *Research on educational innovations* (2nd ed.). Larchmont, NY: Eye On Education.

Goble, P. (1991). *Iktomi and the buffalo skull.* New York: Scholastic.

Goldberg, M. F. (1990). Portrait of Madeline Hunter. *Educational Leadership 47* (5),141–143.

Good, T. L., & Brophy, J. E. (2000). *Looking in classrooms* (8th ed.). New York: Addison-Wesley.

Jarolimek, J., Foster, Sr., C. D., & Kellough, R. D. (2005). *Teaching and learning in the elementary school* (8th ed.). Upper Saddle River, NJ: Merrill/Prentice Hall.

Joyce, B., Weil, M., & Calhoun, E. (2000). *Models of teaching* (6th ed.). Boston: Allyn & Bacon.

Kauchak, D. P., & Eggen, P. D. (2007). *Learning and teaching: Research-based methods* (5th ed.). Boston: Allyn & Bacon.

Kellough, R. D., & Roberts, P. L. (2002). *A resource guide for elementary school teaching: Planning for competence* (5th ed.). Upper Saddle River, NJ: Merrill/Prentice Hall.

Marchesani, R. J. (2007). *The field guide to teaching: A handbook for new teachers.* Upper Saddle River, NJ: Merrill/Prentice Hall.

Marzano, R. J., Norford, J. S., Paynter, D. E., Pickering, D. J., & Gaddy, B. B. (2001). *A handbook for classroom instruction that works.* Alexandria, VA: Association for Supervision and Curriculum Development.

Marzano, R. J., Pickering, D. J., & Pollock, J. E. (2001). *Classroom instruction that works: Research-based strategies for increasing student achievement.* Alexandria, VA: Association for Supervision and Curriculum Development.

Meyer, L. A. (1984). Long-term academic effects of the Direct Instruction Project follow-through. *Elementary School Journal, 84,* 380–394.

Morrison, G. S. (2000). *Teaching in America* (2nd ed.). Needham Heights, MA: Allyn & Bacon.

National Research Council. (2000). *How people learn: Brain, mind, experience, and school* (expanded ed.). Washington, D.C.: National Academy Press.

Pallotta, J. (1993). *The extinct alphabet book.* Watertown, MA: Charlesbridge Publishing.

Pallotta, J. (2002). *The skull alphabet book.* Watertown, MA: Charlesbridge Publishing.

Pasch, M., Langer, G., Gardner, T. G., Starko, A. J., & Moody, C. D. (1995). *Teaching as decision making: Successful practices for the elementary teacher* (3rd ed.). White Plains, NY: Longman.

Salsbury, D. E. (2002). Comparing teacher-directed and computer-assisted instruction of elementary geographic place vocabulary [Dissertation]. Manhattan, KS: Kansas State University.

Smith, B. A. (1986). The effect of two instructional methods intended to improve the place vocabulary of middle school students [Dissertation]. Athens, GA: University of Georgia.

Smith, B. A. (1997). Social studies teacher's companion. Boston: Houghton Mifflin.

Sousa, D. A. (2001). *How the brain learns* (2nd ed.). Thousand Oaks, CA: Corwin Press.

Starko, A. J., Sparks-Langer, G. M., Pasch, M., Frankes, L., Gardner, T. G., & Moody, C. D. (2003). *Teaching as decision making: Successful practices for the elementary teacher* (3rd ed.). Upper Saddle River, NJ: Merrill/Prentice Hall.

Tomlinson, C. A. (1999–2000). *The differentiated classroom.* Alexandria, VA: Association for Supervision and Curriculum Development.

World Almanac for Kids. (2006). Amazing animal facts. Retrieved December, 2006, from http://www.worldalmanacforkids.com/explore/animals.html.

Name Index

Animal Planet, 124
Armstrong, T., 104
Ausubel, D., 35
Ayers, W., 9

Bain, A., 102
Bainer, D., 61
Barbour, N., 24
Bates, E., 11
Bean, R., 12
Bereiter, C., 102
Bess, J., 82
Bialo, E., 103
Bittel, L. R., 6
Black, P., 65, 66
Blanton, S., 135
Bloom, B. S., 51
Boggiano, B. K., 83
Boster, F. J., 102
Brandt, R., 63, 82
Bransford, J. D., 120
Brookfield, S. D., 23
Brooks, J., 25
Brooks, M., 25
Brophy, J., 10, 132
Brown, A. L., 120
Brown, J., 86, 103
Brubaker, D. L., 23–24
Burden, P. R., 7, 34, 36, 103, 104, 121
Byrd, D. M., 7, 34, 36, 103, 104, 121

Calhoun, E., 131
California Reading Task Force, 37, 38
Center for Learning and Technology, 131
Chall, J. S., 116, 117–118
Clark, C., 7, 23
Clinton, J. C., 23
Cocking, R. R., 120
Confucius, 91, 131
Cooter, R. B., 102
Cotton, K., 103, 121, 122
Council of Chief State School Officers, 4, 25, 26, 27, 28, 89
Cradler, J., 103
Cradler, R., 103
Cruickshank, D., 61
Crump, A. D., 26

Dale, E., 90
Dana, J. C., 77
Daniels, H., 7

Davidson Institute for Talent Development, 79
Dewey, J., 23, 118
DiScipio, T., 86
DiVesta, F., 131
Doolittle, P. E., 25

EdSource, 10
Eggen, P. D., 7, 34, 35, 49, 117, 118, 121, 123
Elliott, D. L., 34
Ellis, A. K., 117
Emerson, R. W., 121
Engelhart, M. D., 51
Evans, D. N., 39

Fan, X., 26
Florida Department of Education, 53
Foster, C., 61, 87, 116
Fouts, J. T., 117
Franklin, B., 46
Fulmer, D., 12
Furst, E. J., 51

Gaddy, B. B., 131
Gardner, H., 64, 83–85, 104
Geddis, A. N., 28
Geography Education Standards Project, 37
Ginott, H., 21
Goble, P., 124
Goldberg, M. F., 118
Goleman, D., 27–28
Good, T. L., 132
Gronlund, N., 50
Grumet, J., 12

Hattie, J., 23, 61
Hepburn, K. S., 106
Hill, W. H., 51
Hyde, A., 7

Indiana Department of Education, 47
Inge, C. C., 102
International Reading Association, 53

Jacobsen, D., 49, 50
Jarolimek, J., 61, 63, 87, 116, 117, 131
Jones, L. S., 11
Jones, V. F., 11
Joyce, B., 131

Kaestle, C. F., 4
Katz, L., 78

Subject Index